THE BEST IN

EXHIBITION
STAND DESIGN:2

THE BEST IN

EXHIBITION
STAND DESIGN:2

STAFFORD CLIFF

ROTOVISION

A QUARTO BOOK

Published by ROTOVISION SA
Route Suisse 9
CH-1295 Mies
Switzerland

ISBN 2-88046-233-9

This book was designed and produced by
Quarto Publishing plc
6 Blundell Street
London N7 9BH

Consultant Editor: Stafford Cliff
Project Manager: Katie Bland
Designer: James Lawrence

Typeset in Great Britain by
Central Southern Typesetters, Eastbourne
Manufactured in Singapore by ProVision Pty
Printed in China by
Leefung-Asco Printers Ltd

Stafford Cliff would like to acknowledge
the help of the following people
in the compilation of this book :
Jonathan Scott, Katie Bland, Sophie Hutchinson,
Wayne Newell, Peter Higgins and Stephen Paul.

Contents

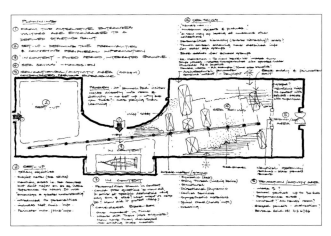

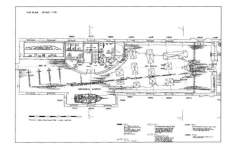

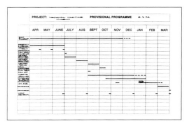

TOP **An important part of the credentials presentation for the National Maritime project included a series of sketch plans showing how the space was to be divided by a timber 'breakwater'. In the second plan, consideration is given to the flow of traffic, through areas labelled entry space etc. In the third version, the cut-away ship was abandoned, but the Education Activities area became an important classroom facility**

ABOVE LEFT AND ABOVE **A very sketchy visual, and the first provisional programme, finishing with 'contractor on site'**

Introduction by Stafford Cliff

Where do Exhibition designers come from? What sort of training and qualifications do they have? How do they work, where do they get their ideas from, how long does it take and what stages does a design go through?

Having selected the work for this, the second edition of **The Best in Exhibition Stand Design** that I have edited, I thought it might be interesting to take two examples of very different exhibition stands and talk to the designers responsible – to find out.

Wayne Newell, who's dynamic group, Innervisions, have created a number of the trade shows in this book, studied arts and sciences at school. At the end of his foundation course at Twickenham art school, he considered both architecture and interior design. It was his tutor who suggested that he try an exhibition design course. From the first day, he never had any doubts about it. "It suddenly clicked. It contained the things I was already interested in, plus the pleasure of seeing your work realised quickly." The course combined the creative and the practical, dealing with the preparation of visuals and models, designing in two and three dimensions, and the solid practicalities of structure and materials.

He graduated in 1980. It was the start of the boom in design. The students on his course had been encouraged to visit exhibition contractors, and all seven found jobs within the first six months. "In my first job I really found out how things were built, on tight schedules and for demanding clients. It was good experience in all the practical aspects – planning, preparation, budgeting and construction".

At the end of 1982, he formed the company that was to become Innervisions. "I was twenty-two years old. I started by doing visuals for established contractors. In the first month I made £127. Then I began looking at exhibitions and contacting companies – small ones at first".

"I heard that RCA-Columbia Pictures were looking for someone to design a stand for their home entertainment division. It was absurdly ambitious but I pitched for it anyway. I drew on everything I had learned: I made a big model and presented it as confidently as I could. The presentation was to the managing director, Steve Bernard, I'll always be grateful that he decided to give me the chance".

The job was successful and led to a two-year continuous programme. Bernard was in charge of launching a video disc product and he contracted Innervisions to control his trade shows strategy.

In those days, Newell worked on his own, building on that first break and accumulating experience and establishing his reputation. "I did mostly public shows, especially for the electronics industry. I had desk space in a small office, and I worked twenty-four hours a day".

Now Innervisions works out of an office in London's Regent's Park and employs seven people. The creative side is the heart of the business, of course – four of the seven are designers – but Newell gives a high priority to effective selling. This is in the hands of Bridget Harrison, Innervisions' very full-time marketing director. "More work doesn't automatically follow a successful job. You have to go out and sell. No matter how busy we are, we maintain a steady, energetic marketing campaign. We have very good sales people, and we re-issue our brochure every two years. Unless you create the opportunity to design, you don't design. And if you stand still, you find that other people start copying you".

On the other side of town, in an industrial space beside a pleasant tree-lined square, behind a post office, up some industrial metal steps, is the studio of Land Design, who specialise in exhibition design of a very different kind.

Peter Higgins is one of the three partners.

He started as an architect working at the BBC – not on architecture but on sets for film dramas. He designed exhibitions and sets for product launches on a freelance basis and 'moonlighted' in the West End Theatre world. He then took a job as senior designer at Imagination, one of Europe's largest exhibition and presentation specialists – where he met his other partners, James Dibble and Shirley Walker, both interior designers who had crossed over into other divisions of the business.

"We got a lot of confidence and we worked to a very high standard of finish. We also gained some business acumen and thought that one day we'd like to have our own business – but weren't sure what. Our ambition was to do permanent exhibitions." In 1992 they founded Land Design Studio. Peter left Imagination first and the other two followed.

"We have six people full-time – four 3-D designers, one graphic designer (Junia Brown), and one administrative, but we put together a team, job-by-job, like a film crew. We'll usually have a production manager, a producer/ account handler, a lighting designer, a sound designer and possibly an audiovisual specialist".

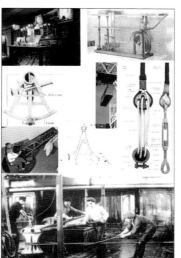

The three partners handle all the new business and when recently, the National Maritime Museum at Greenwich in London asked them to pitch for a major new gallery space, they were given just two weeks to gather their thoughts and come up with some ideas.

Five agencies were in competition for the job and each was asked to present their credentials and a small document that included some notional plans – some ideas that were later used, and some that were not.

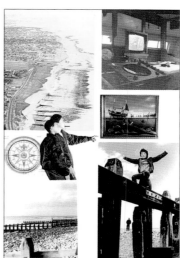

ABOVE **The atmosphere of the exhibition was conveyed by collages of cuttings, archive material and snaps of some of the exhibits. One board (top) clearly shows the inspiration for the central spine**

But the Project Director at the National Maritime, Hélène Mitchell, liked their 'Modus Operandi' and they got the job. There was no budget at this stage but the team worked on a fee structure based on a percentage of what it would cost to build the exhibition, including all the graphics.

The brief was to provide 7–11 year old children with an imaginative interactive facility that would introduce many aspects of seafaring whilst

ABOVE **A series of tiny card and paper models, were created by the designers to experiment with shapes and show the client how the five Interactive modules might look**

BELOW **The final plan of the space, projected into axonametric. Visitors enter on the right and progress towards a central area of exhibits designed to demonstrate the basic skills with 'hands-on' apparatus**

incorporating relevant museum artifacts. Ultimately, the object of the gallery was to set a context for the 'journey' through the main body of the museum nearby. It became known as 'The All Hands Gallery'.

Since its audience was children, the designers immediately started working with educationalists from the museum, as well as the curator and a writer. Over a series of weekly meetings, the solution took shape. One element in the original sketch plans that remained was a long spine that divided the difficult rectangular space, and provided a structure to the exhibition and a way of regulating traffic flow. It took the form of a stylised timber breakwater.

Peter and Shirley went beach combing and put together a collage board of all sorts of seaside elements. They also produced mood boards and lots of rough sketches, and tiny sketch models, rather than detailed perspective drawings. The brief kept developing and much energy was spent on trying to define what the gallery wanted to say and the best way to say it.

Role-play became important, children would be accompanied by 'enablers' and would work in teams, particularly in the first section, where five themed modules encourage children to learn about specific seafarers, from the Viking to the modern yachtswoman. It was an important part of the brief too, to define which objects were 'real' and which were fabricated 'hands on' re-creations.

Another major element of the show, is the enormous $\frac{1}{16}$th scale model of H.M.S. Cornwallis which had to be slid in through a gallery window. Along the five fins of the breakwater, children learn about gunnery, cargo, pilotage, diving, propulsion and signalling.

Last but not least, a logo-type was needed to give the new gallery a recognisable image.

Junia Brown worked on all the graphics for the exhibition and when it came to the logo, he thought immediately of "manning the yardarm" as an idea. He gave this brief to three different illustrators to interpret, but ultimately it just didn't work.

In the end, an etching by Gustave Doré from 'The Ancient Mariner' was adapted and stylised to become three sailors pulling together.

BELOW **The logo evolved from an original etching by Gustave Doré, into a stylised but no less evocative symbol of the spirit of seafaring**

"Every exhibition needs it own identity, it's incredibly important – in fact I did it first, before all the rest of the graphics," he said.

The exhibition was opened by the Duke of Edinburgh, on 6th April 1995 and is planned to last seven to ten years.

This contrasts with the style and pace of the trade fairs where Innervisions do their best work. Many stands last only a few days, though nowadays they are increasingly required to be reusable. Modular design enables them to travel to different fairs, and even to be rebuilt to different sizes and shapes.

The trade fair world is highly competitive, and Innervisions regularly pitch for new contracts. The presentation may just be credentials, sometimes it is paid creative work, but sometimes a free pitch is required. Innervisions go to see all prospective clients, but they are very selective when it comes to pitching. "Presentations absorb a great deal of time and effort, so we'd rather not do it at all than be half-hearted. We make very comprehensive presentations, with high-quality models and visuals, and full documentation, because we think that's the best way to explain our approach. Presentations therefore consume substantial resources, but the upshot is that we have a very good hit rate." In fact, they win four out of every five jobs they go for.

In the case of the Microsoft project, Newell had been working for the client for four years so he knew them well. He knew all the physical aspects of the stand and he knew the product. But this time, he needed a "big idea – the 'wow factor' ".

Innervisions' head designer, François Nouyou, was encouraged to take a radical approach. Since the whole show was being run by Microsoft, their own stand could be flexible about some of the limitations.

There were strict practical requirements that had to be addressed first, however. The stand had to be open and accessible, and it had to be extremely efficient from a business perspective. When looking at the pictures in these pages, readers of this book may sometimes not realise to what an extent such issues determine a design. "We may get excited about the architecture," points out

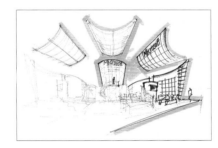

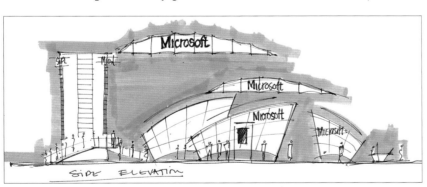

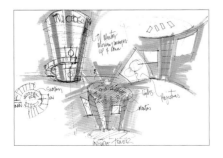

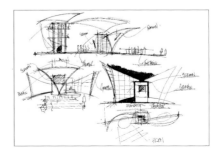

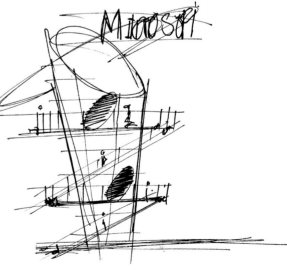

LEFT AND ABOVE **Some of the designer's initial 'scribbles' clearly show how the tower was to be linked to the rest of the stand, with a strong feeling for geometry and structural balance**

 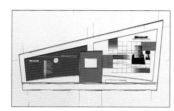

ABOVE **Boards from the first presentation show the theatre area, and how the clear approach to graphics was co-ordinated across all the modules**

Newell "but the clients' priority is that the stand should relate successfully to the product and the corporation".

Thus, although much of Innervisions work is involved with special effects – moving message technology, the creation of a theatrical atmosphere – the 'action-packed' approach is underpinned by a fundamental understanding of the marketing requirements. Innervisions' response is to fit in with the client's brief, but to move a little ahead of it – to respect it, but to enhance it, too.

The solution to the Microsoft project derived, in fact, from an analysis of the functions of the various areas of the stand, the space planning and the need to maximise what the exhibition industry calls 'the footfall' – the number of visitors to the stand. Newell is emphatic. "What it's all about is efficiency".

The design team had three weeks to prepare the initial concepts. Because they knew the client, they decided the best way to present their ideas was in the form of a computer-animated 'walk-through' of the entire stand.

But first, Newell and his team talked through the brief, then let it ferment while they got on with other work. A week later, they sat down together again and discussed ideas, some as scribbled visuals, some of them simply verbal. While the design team were pushing at the creative limits, Newell, whose task it would be to present the result, helped to keep them within the boundaries of what could be achieved. "Ideas need to be practical".

It was decided that the stand would have a strong pictorial content, it would incorporate a lot of projection and there would be a computer-animated graphic system. There would be both theatre-style and one-on-one demonstrations where visitors could 'test-drive' the product. Boldest of all, at the centre of the stand there would be a 12m high tower – something never done before at a trade exhibition. "Suddenly a whole lot of new possibilities were opened up. We could use drop-screen techniques, we could raise and lower the audience and rotate them 360 degrees as part of a multimedia demonstration".

The stand opened on 28th February 1995 at London's Olympia show complex. It formed the key to the client's corporate exhibitions strategy for the following three years. There would be twenty-five to thirty shows a year, as frequently as every week during the autumn months. Innervisions handled them all, adapting the stand to sites ranging in size from 12 to 1,500 square metres. All variants followed the same fundamental design, and sufficient components were made for them all.

For the eight-week production programme, Innervisions assembled a team of twelve key suppliers who worked full time, right through Christmas. They included specialist contractors for steel-working and carpentry, lighting, special effects and audiovisuals.

The public queued for up to two and a half hours to get into the tower presentation.

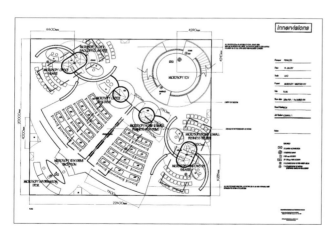

ABOVE **The planning of the space had to take into account a large area devoted to demonstrating the computer programmes**

And afterwards? Newell never goes to the 'rip-outs' nowadays. "It's too heart-breaking." Increasingly, though, as with the Microsoft stand, the task includes storing and re-erecting reuseable components rather than just throwing them away after the show. "It's a question of sound economics; companies often need elements that can be changed and updated, modified so that they can be used at consumer as well as trade venues, and so on".

And ideas – where do they come from? Wayne Newell gets input from his contractors – a lighting technician will come to him with a new piece of equipment he has developed, possibly from a theatre project.

Innervisions develop close working relation-

ABOVE **Frames from the computer generated 'walk-through' video, bring to 3-D life, the architectural aspects and demonstrate how the various modules will look, particularly the swooping ceiling panels**

ships with their specialist suppliers, and will sponsor them to develop fittings and techniques to solve particular problems.

"Everything's been done before," says Newell; "it's *how* you do it that counts".

For Peter Higgins at Land Design Studio – his colleagues say "he never switches off!" He learns a lot from the theatre and from film – Robert Lepage and Laurie Anderson in the theatre, Francis Ford Coppola in the cinema and the architect Frederick Kiesler – "people who cross the disciplines – break the rules".

He and Wayne Newell should meet.

ABOVE **In a series of candid snaps taken during the five day build-up of the stand, the vast space (550m²) is quickly filled by the central tower, and then the information desk and surrounding units**

Forty people were employed full-time, so everything had to be carefully planned and co-ordinated, with each contractor's efforts fitting together, and as much constructed off-site as possible

Innervisions also designed the special seating and demonstration consoles

All Hands Gallery

DATE & LOCATION: 1995 April, The National Maritime Museum, Greenwich, London

TARGET AUDIENCE: General public, particularly 7-11 year old children

TYPE OF STAND: Permanent

SIZE (SQUARE METRES OR FEET): 350m

STAND MANUFACTURER : After Design

DESIGNER: Land Design Studio Ltd, London, England

CLIENT'S BRIEF: To provide 7-11 year olds with an interactive facility that would intro duce many aspects of seafaring, whilst incorporating relevant museum artifacts. The ultimate objective of this gallery is to set a context for the journey through the main body of the museum.

DESIGN RATIONALE: The starting point was the installation of a stylised timber breakwater that would define an architectural spine within an otherwise awkward space. The first area presents five themed modules that investigate specific seafarers. Utilising carefully selected historical clues, these compact sculptural units describe a range of characters from the Viking through to the modern yachtswoman. As a complimentary experience the next area continues the theatrical approach combined with more sophisticated technology. This encourages the visitor to participate in key seafaring activities such as gunnery, cargo handling and even a deep sea diving simulator. Land's design methodology has been to combine an architectural approach with theatrical interpretation and quality interior design finishes as a solution to exhibition design.

Microsoft/Windows '95

DATE & LOCATION: 1995 February-March, London, England

TARGET AUDIENCE: Influential end-users

TYPE OF STAND: Temporary

SIZE (SQUARE): 550m

DESIGNER: Innervisions Interiors & Exhibitions Ltd

CLIENT'S BRIEF: To create a platform for Microsoft's products and applications. To provide a dramatic theatrical environment for a preview of a Microsoft vision of the future whilst ensuring a maximum audience interest

DESIGN RATIONALE: A series of open theatres and hands-on test drives focused around a 12m high circular tower which contained a spectacular interactive presentation. This featured 140 monitors, drop screens and pre-programmed light and laser show

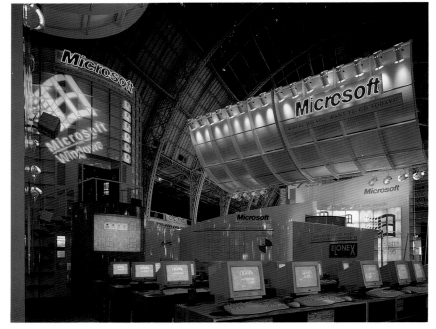

(continued from p.15, Microsoft/Windows '95, Innervisions Interiors & Exhibitions Ltd)

CHAPTER ONE

GALLERIES

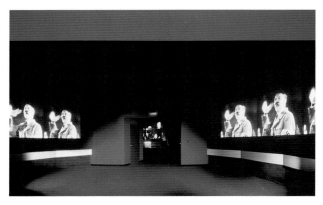

Human Intolerance and its Consequence

DATE & LOCATION: 1993, Museum of Tolerance, Los Angeles, USA

TARGET AUDIENCE: Young multiethnic Americans

TYPE OF STAND: Permanent

SIZE (SQUARE METRES OR FEET): 2,500m

DESIGNER: James Gardner 3D Concepts Ltd, London, England

CLIENT'S BRIEF: To increase awareness of contemporary issues of prejudice within the American experience, as a prelude to describing events in Europe of 50 years ago

DESIGN RATIONALE: The museum is divided into two distinct halves. The first, a lively interactive workshop with a free-flow circulation and participatory exhibits designed to reveal 'hidden' prejudices. The mood changes when visitors enter the stark, monochromatic atmosphere of the second section – a timed walk-through European history from 1919 to 1945. The Holocaust section is made of a six screen audiovisual theatre showing multiple images of the Hitler Youth movement and Nuremburg Rallies. Gates and tunnels with video monitors encased in concrete, show footage of concentration camps. A searchlight is activated to scan the perimeter fence

'Broken Lines'

DATE & LOCATION: 1993 April–June, The Kruithuis
Museum of Technology, Hertogembosch,
Netherlands

TARGET AUDIENCE: General public

TYPE OF STAND: Travelling

DESIGNER: Opera Ruimtelijk Ontwerpers, Amsterdam,
The Netherlands

CLIENT'S BRIEF: Retrospective of Emmy van Leersum's
work, one of Holland's major of contemporary
jewellery makers

DESIGN RATIONALE: Each exhibition unit consists of a
vertical glass sheet, the central element, supports
both the objects to be displayed and the
accompanying text and visuals. The sheet is
supported by a heavy steel base. Display elements
of wood and steel, attached to the edge of the
glass sheet, provide the packaging cases for the
objects during transport, this system offers great
flexibility. Lighting is integrated

Cycloramas: Summer Olympic games & Winter Olympic games

DATE & LOCATION: 1993 June, official opening of Olympic Museum, Lausanne, Switzerland

TARGET AUDIENCE: General public

TYPE OF STAND: Permanent

SIZE (SQUARE METRES OR FEET): Total exhibition surfaces of the Olympic museum: 3,300m

DESIGNER: Jorge Agostoni, Iker Larauri, Luis Monréal, Jean-Françoise Pahud/Muséographica Mexico and Créations publicitaires Moser SA, Switzerland

CLIENT'S BRIEF: An old dream of the President of the International Olympic Committee, Mr. Juanantonio Samaranch, was to realise the idea of the founder of the IOC, Baron Pierre de Coubertin

DESIGN RATIONALE: Highlights of the Olympics are screened on a wall of television monitors. Historical to contemporary artifacts, from all Olympic sports exhibited in chronological order, are set against white backdrops

The Environment Theatre

DATE & LOCATION: 1993 September, The National Museum of Natural Science, Taichung, Taiwan

TARGET AUDIENCE: General public

TYPE OF STAND: Permanent

SIZE (METRES OR FEETSQUARE): 500m

DESIGNER: MET Studio Ltd, London, England

CLIENT'S BRIEF: To provide a single audiovisual installation that would offer visitors a spectacular glimpse of the natural world. The theatre had to appeal to all age groups and to be flexible enough to allow for the changing needs of the museum

DESIGN RATIONALE: Theatrical and exhibition techniques are used to create a unique 360 degree vision. Computers are used to manipulate and harmonise images and enable precise control of the spectacular multilayered installation. The infrastructure is designed so that the museum can renew presentations at a minimum cost

PHOTOGRAPHER: Niall Clutton

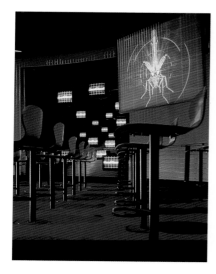

Evolution House

DATE & LOCATION: 1995 July, Kew Gardens, England

TARGET AUDIENCE: General public

TYPE OF STAND: Permanent

SIZE (SQUARE METRES OR FEET): 420m

DESIGNER: Alan Ward/MET Studio Ltd, London, England

STAND MANUFACTURER: Logiclord & Electrosonic, England

CLIENT'S BRIEF: To look at the evolution of plant life through 3,500 million years in a way that would be sympathetic to the environment

DESIGN RATIONALE: Display units fabricated from copper were moulded to suggest plant forms. High suspended sound cones give a voice-over narrative and background sound effects are played to enrich the atmosphere such as distant thunder and volcanic activity. The interpretation reaches a climax inside a spectacular cave, where the specially commissioned glass engraving of a magnolia forms a centre piece. Scenic painting and special lighting complement the displays

GLASS ENGRAVER: Radford & Ball

PHOTOGRAPHER: Marcus Hilton

Powerhouse Museum

DATE & LOCATION: 1987, Powerhouse Museum, Sydney, Australia

TARGET AUDIENCE: Visitors to the museum

TYPE OF STAND: Permanent

DESIGNER: Garry Emery/Emery Vincent Design, Sydney, Australia

CLIENT'S BRIEF: To provide an innovative solution to display a list of museum sponsors

DESIGN RATIONALE: The design solution is intended to have multiple readings so the result maintained the identity of the museum. The entrance of the museum in itself an exhibit

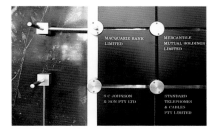

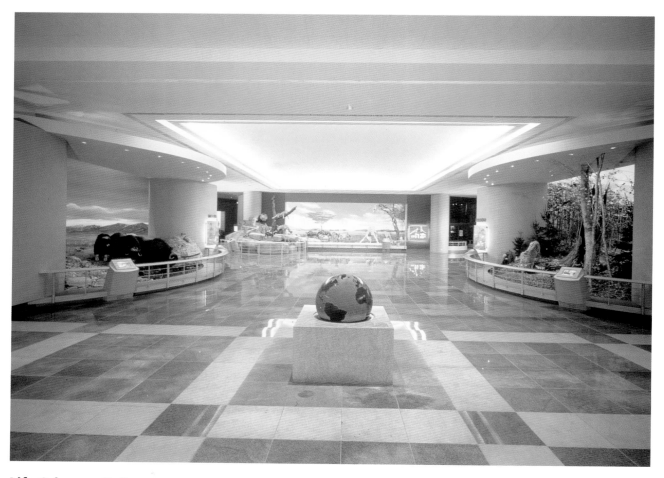

Life Sciences Gallery

DATE & LOCATION: 1993 September, National Museum of
Natural Science, 1 Kuan Chien Road, Taichung,
Taiwan, ROC

TARGET AUDIENCE: General public

TYPE OF STAND: Permanent

SIZE (SQUARE METRES OR FEET): 1,500m

DESIGNER: MET Studio Ltd, London, England

CLIENT'S BRIEF: To design an exhibition displaying seven
of the world's natural habitats and examining the
inter-relationship between all living things using
traditional diorama techniques. The space was to
serve a dual function as a theatre for museum and
as a space for corporate entertainment

DESIGN RATIONALE: MET Studio reinterpreted the
traditional into modern form by blending
multimedia techniques with the long established
craft of creating dioramas involving the
international coordination of craftspeople. The
result is dramatic and elegant whilst being
scientifically accurate

Science for Life

DATE & LOCATION: 1995, Wellcome Trust, London, England

TARGET AUDIENCE: Science students, general public

TYPE OF STAND: Permanent

SIZE (SQUARE METRES OR FEET): 750m

DESIGNER: MET Studio Ltd, London, England

CLIENT'S BRIEF: To create an exhibition on medical research as the centre piece of its new initiative, 'The Wellcome Centre for Medical Science'. A lively and modern approach to excite and inform was top priority. To give visitors a greater understanding of the benefits of bio-medical research and the need to sustain funding

DESIGN RATIONALE: A sophisticated, elegant space features custom built interactives with computer games and audiovisual devices to communicate the excitement of research

PHOTOGRAPHER: Niall Clutton

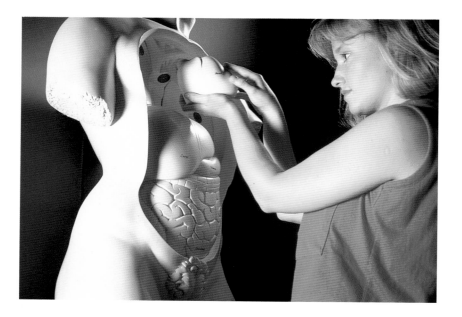

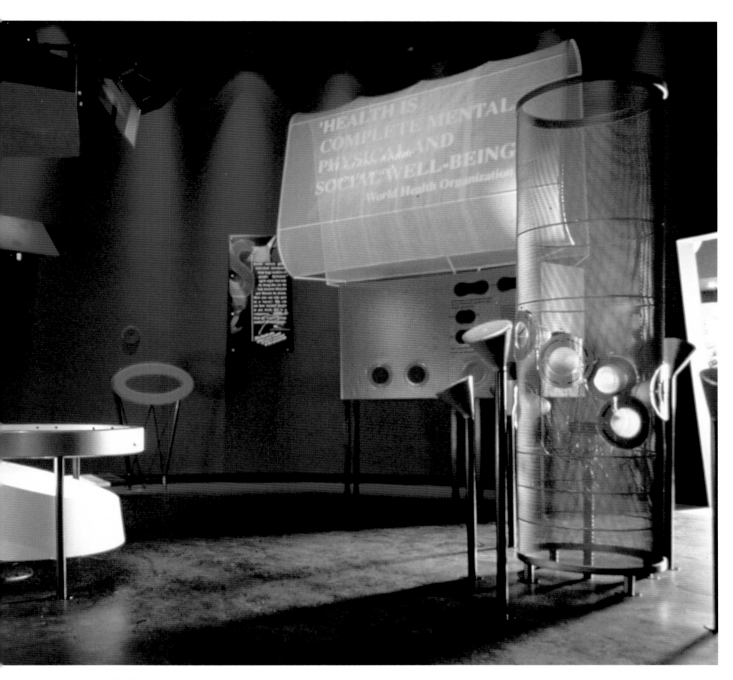

Health Matters

DATE & LOCATION: 1994 July, Science Museum, London, England

TARGET AUDIENCE: General public

TYPE OF STAND: Permanent

DESIGNER: Fitch and Jasper Jacobs Associates, London, England

CLIENT'S BRIEF: To improve public awareness and understanding of modern medicine. To highlight the development of medical technologies, examine lifestyles and disease and open up a world of experimental science from a patient's perspective whilst being exciting and informative

DESIGN RATIONALE: The exhibition was designed around three themes with a number of displays specially commissioned by artists, photographers and automation makers. A unique blend of interactive exhibits, audiovisual communication and medical artefacts

Seapower in the Twentieth Century

DATE & LOCATION: 1992 September, National Maritime Museum, Greenwich, London, England

TARGET AUDIENCE: General public

TYPE OF STAND: Permanent

SIZE (SQUARE METRES OR FEET): 500m

DESIGNER: David Fraser/Fitch, London, England

CLIENT'S BRIEF: To design an exhibition celebrating 100 years of naval achievement

DESIGN RATIONALE: Fitch designed a mould-breaking exhibition gallery which established a balance between traditional display and full blown 'experience', illustrating key events in twentieth century history set against the technological advances which characterised those events

ADDITIONAL CREDITS: Chris Gascoigne

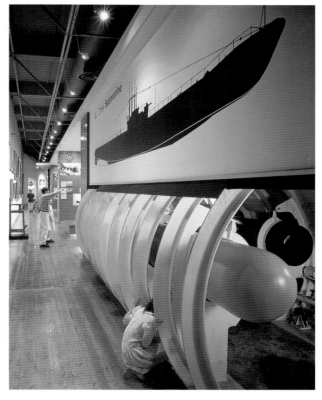

'Keep out of the Cold . . . Clothing for Arctic Dwellers'

DATE & LOCATION: 1993 October–1994 April, National Museum of Ethnology, Leiden, The Netherlands

TARGET AUDIENCE: General public

TYPE OF STAND: Temporary

SIZE (SQUARE METRES OR FEET): 550m

DESIGNER: Opera Ruimtellijk Ontwerpers, Amsterdam, The Netherlands

CLIENT'S BRIEF: To provide an insight into the Arctic dweller's way of living and their relation to the climate and natural surroundings

DESIGN RATIONALE: The clothing itself was exhibited on horizontal, transparent sheets of glass, lit from below. This risky method of display was chosen because it reduced the distance between the objects and the viewer to a minimum. Moving three-dimensional illustrations, showing scenes from the life of the arctic people and animals were seen from above and beneath a simulated sheet of ice

ILLUSTRATOR: Berry van Gerwen

Treasure Chamber

DATE & LOCATION: 1991, Rotterdam Maritime Museum,
The Netherlands

TARGET AUDIENCE: General public

TYPE OF STAND: Permanent

DESIGNER: René van Raalte/BRS Premsela Vonk,
Amsterdam, The Netherlands

CLIENT'S BRIEF: To house the museum's valuable
collection in an air conditioned and isolated area

DESIGN RATIONALE: A curved ramp leads the visitor to
the entrance. Each showcase containing the item
was air conditioned. The chamber is elevated to
express the character of the exhibit. A solemn
atmosphere is created by the careful use of light

Jacobsen Review Gallery

DATE & LOCATION: 1994 June, Design Museum, London, England

TARGET AUDIENCE: General public

TYPE OF STAND: Temporary

DESIGNER: Ian Cartlidge/Cartlidge Levene, London, England

CLIENT'S BRIEF: To produce graphics and supporting captions for Arne Jacobsen's work, around a pre-designed layout

DESIGN RATIONALE: A more interactive space was created by adding graphics to the outer walls which explained Jacobsen's Life in a chronological order detailing his achievements

Review Gallery, Design Museum

DATE & LOCATION: 1990–1995, Review Gallery, Design Museum, London, England

TARGET AUDIENCE: General public

TYPE OF STAND: Permanent

DESIGNERS: Simon Browning, Yumi Matote, Sean Perkins/Cartlidge Levene, London, England

CLIENT'S BRIEF: To create a design presence without dominating the surrounding space using typography and light. The gallery is a continually evolving display of new products and prototypes from around the world

DESIGN RATIONALE: A central screen using type as texture creates a focal point for the exhibitions

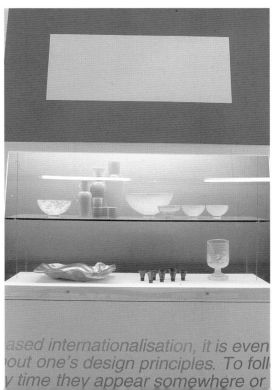

ased internationalisation, it is even
out one's design principles. To foll
y time they appear somewhere or

North Sea Exhibition

DATE & LOCATION: 1989, Museum of Education,
The Hague, The Netherlands

TARGET AUDIENCE: General public

TYPE OF STAND: Permanent

SIZE (SQUARE METRES OR FEET): 120m

STAND MANUFACTURER: Vormgeversatelier, Rotterdam

DESIGNER: René van Raalte/BRS Premsela Vonk,
Amsterdam, The Netherlands

CLIENT'S BRIEF: To create an educational exhibition
based on the 'North Sea Experience'

DESIGN RATIONALE: Different types of weather were
simulated, the shipping information is displayed on
a moving platform so that the visitor takes the
place of a helmsman. Marine life is presented in an
open display with live sea animals which one can
touch

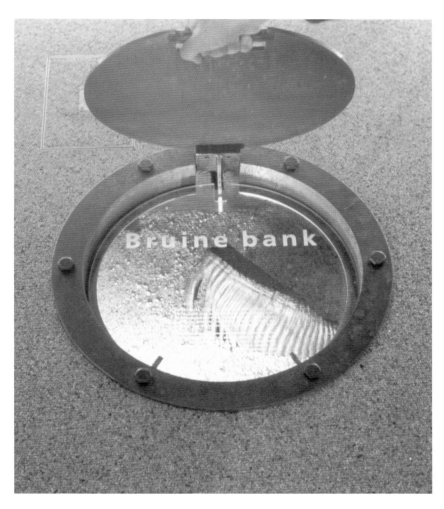

The Architecture of New Prague

DATE & LOCATION: 1995 October–December, World Financial Center, New York, USA

TARGET AUDIENCE: General public

TYPE OF STAND: Temporary

DESIGNERS: Stephen Doyle, William Drenttel, Gary Tooth, Rosemarie Turk/Drenttel Doyle Partners, New York, USA

CLIENT'S BRIEF: To reflect the complex web of architectural styles in Prague which historically is a centre of culture and art

DESIGN RATIONALE: The installation used the design of a room within a room to convey the sense of being on the outside looking in. The interior room, constructed of plywood with architectural images symmetrically applied, contained tall and narrow openings allowing visitors a glimpse of the panoramic cityscape. A detached blue entrance structure was distorted to create a modern passageway leading to a visual reflection of a city

ARCHITECTURE: Miguel Oks

PHOTOGRAPHY: Scot Frances/Esto

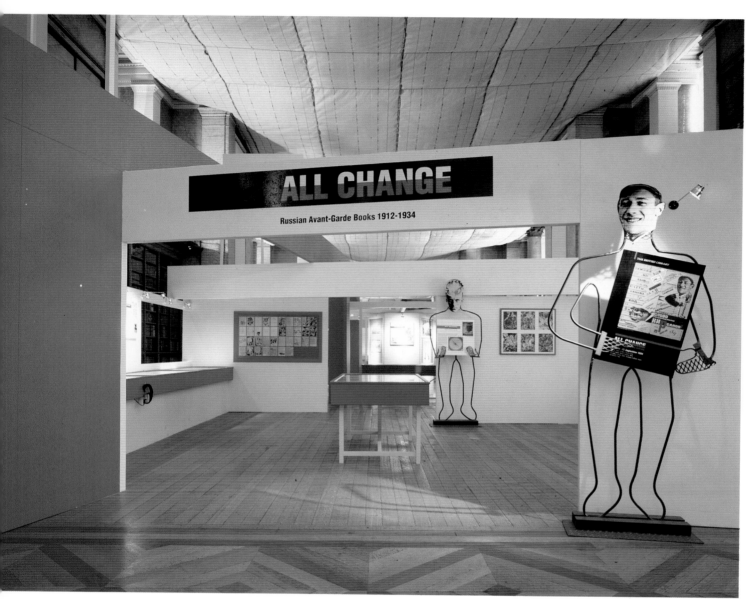

All-Change, Russian Avant-garde Books 1912–1934

DATE & LOCATION: 1994 June–September, The British Library, London, England

TARGET AUDIENCE: General public

TYPE OF STAND: Temporary

DESIGNER: Andrew Feast, Nigel Gray/Carter Wong & Partners, London, England

CLIENT'S BRIEF: To create a space within the King's Library to display the extensive collection of Russian Avant-garde books

DESIGN RATIONALE: To reflect the historical content and in response to the space, a reconstruction of Rodchenko's Workers' Reading Room was the focus for the display of the books. This was set amongst a vast free-standing constructivist composition of planes and volumes linked by a curved wall painted in rich red

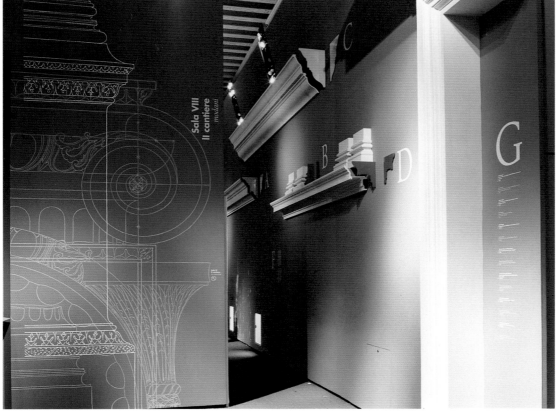

Renaissance, the Performance of Architecture

DATE & LOCATION: 1994, Palazzo Grassi, Venice, Italy

TARGET AUDIENCE: General public

TYPE OF STAND: One-off

DESIGNER: Mario Bellini/Italo Lupi, Milan, Italy

CLIENT'S BRIEF: To celebrate Italian architecture using the entire Palace

DESIGN RATIONALE: Authentic Italian Renaissance architectural wooden models and a giant model of Saint Peter in Rome, 8 metres high, were displayed. The walls were hung with drawings and graphics

Science in the Eighteenth Century

DATE & LOCATION: 1992–1993, Palazzo Grassi, Venice, Italy

TARGET AUDIENCE: General public

TYPE OF STAND: One-off

DESIGNER: Alan Irvine, London, England

CLIENT'S BRIEF: The intention of this exhibition was to show by means of his original drawings, the influence and relationship of Leonardo da Vinci with the Venetian painters

DESIGN RATIONALE: The display system was made up of triangular units formed from three panels with one drawing shown on the long side of each unit. The units were capable of being arranged in various combinations and layouts. The aperture panels were colour coded to identify the various categories of drawings; flower studies, anatomical, and architectural. Relevant sculptures and paintings by the great Venetian masters, including Bellini and Giorgioni were also exhibited

Pictures for Fighting Aids

DATE & LOCATION: 1993 December–1994 March, Red Cross and Crescent Museum, Geneva, Switzerland

TARGET AUDIENCE: General public, especially the young

TYPE OF STAND: Temporary

SIZE (SQUARE METRES OR FEET): 250m

DESIGNER: Roger Pfund, Micheline Jacques/Roger Pfund, Switzerland

CLIENT'S BRIEF: To involve artists from a number of countries, to raise general awareness of the worldwide aids epidemic, to assist the victims and promote medical research

DESIGN RATIONALE: The exhibition featured the Belgian artist Micheline Jacques, who pioneered a plastic form of expression and created a multiplicity of eloquent and striking sculptures using nylon fabric which were dyed, sown and assembled. Using this media and those of other artists, the exhibition hoped to make an impact on those who are still unaware of the travesty and encourage support of the cause

Sons of the Sun and Daughters of the Moon

DATE & LOCATION: 1992 April–November, Museum voor Volkenkunde, Museum of Ethnology, Rotterdam, The Netherlands

TARGET AUDIENCE: General public, historians and students

TYPE OF STAND: Permanent

SIZE (SQUARE METRES OR FEET): Approximately 420m, the entire first floor of the museum

DESIGNER: Paulien Hassink, Shigeru Watano/Watano Matsuzaki Communications bv, Amsterdam, The Netherlands

CLIENT'S BRIEF: The exhibits of pottery, textiles and utensils had to be displayed in an historical/ethnological perspective together with general background information

DESIGN RATIONALE: General information on topics covering religion, geography and culture is provided in the form of maps, interactive programmes, pictorial and architectural setups. Against these backgrounds the main exhibits of pottery, textiles and utensils are displayed

Mise en Boîte

DATE & LOCATION: 1995 January–June, Musée des Arts
et Traditions Populaires, Paris, France

TARGET AUDIENCE: General public

TYPE OF STAND: Temporary

DESIGNER: In-house design team

CLIENT'S BRIEF: To show that the world of the tin can is
not just common place, but is also one of high
technology, influenced by its social and cultural
environment

DESIGN RATIONALE: The tins were displayed in small,
square units set into the walls, giving the
impression that they themselves were boxed-in

Pumphouse: People's History Museum

DATE & LOCATION: 1994 May, The National Museum of Labour History, Manchester, England

TARGET AUDIENCE: General public

TYPE OF STAND: Permanent

SIZE (SQUARE METRES OR FEET): 500m

DESIGNER: Nigel Simpkins/Nigel Simpkins Design, Manchester, England

CLIENT'S BRIEF: To provide a permanent home for the Museum's collections and to celebrate 200 years of the lives of working people whilst conserving delicate objects particularly the museum's fine trade union banner collection

DESIGN RATIONALE: Reconstructions give an impressionistic context to objects and displays are open-ended pieces of theatre intended to challenge the visitor. Information is structured on a simple grid arising from a philosophy of ordered flexibility. Objects are framed in heavy steel on which images, text or recessed cases can be attached

The Birmingham Gas Hall

DATE & LOCATION: 1993 October, Birmingham City Art
Gallery, England

TARGET AUDIENCE: General public

TYPE OF STAND: Permanent

SIZE (SQUARE METRES OR FEET): 26m

DESIGNER: Stanton Williams, London, England

CLIENT'S BRIEF: To convert the Gas Hall, a listed
Edwardian Building, into a gallery accommodating
different sized, international art exhibitions

DESIGN RATIONALE: Flexible screens were used for
displaying anything from large sculptures to
antique lace. An efficient storage system allows for
a quick change over of exhibition, this is made of
blockboard. The screens provide a secure surface
onto which paintings can be screw-fixed and
repainted after use

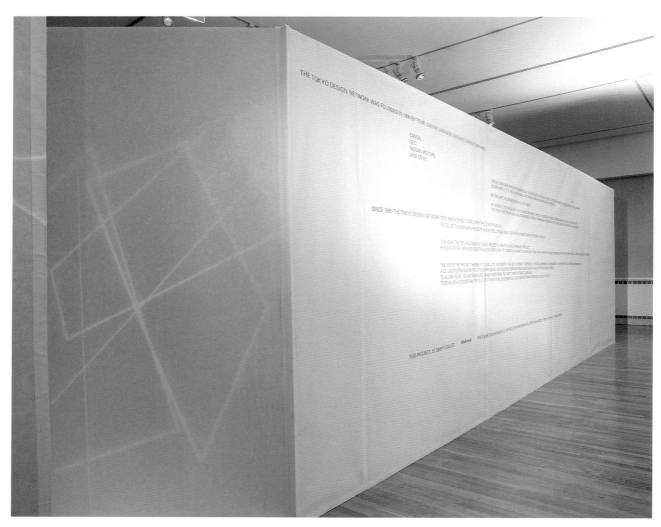

thinkteck/TDN (Tokyo Design Network)

DATE & LOCATION: 1995 March–May, The Design Museum, London, England

TARGET AUDIENCE: General public

TYPE OF STAND: One-off

SIZE (SQUARE METRES OR FEET): 150m

DESIGNER: Ian Cartlidge/Cartlidge Levene, London, England

STAND MANUFACTURER: Design museum's in-house team

CLIENT'S BRIEF: To show how products and their designs have a significant impact on everyday life

DESIGN RATIONALE: The installation was divided into four sections, one for each TDN team, to include texts to illustrate each TDN partner's product. The show case consisted of text-panels, charts, sketches and 3-D models

PHOTOGRAPHER: Alan Calender

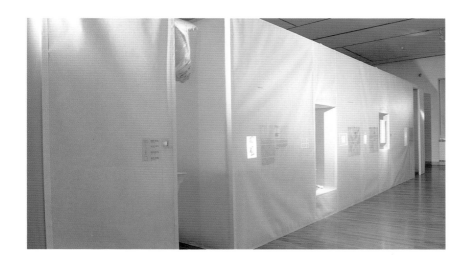

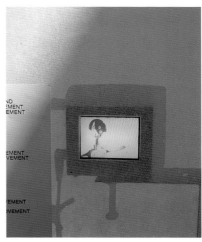

Atsushi Maeda
Styling Design Department
Nissan Motor Co. Ltd.

Daniel Weil (Mentor)
Ross Lovegrove
Jonathan Knight
Shaun Dew

Awareness of each individual moment is what it we are to grasp the intensity of experience. By actively seeking to screen ourselves of the momentary nature of things, our experiences become more vivid and we become less ambivalent about our lives.

I believe this technology must develop in harmony with human desires, and I believe that it can only achieve this by striving to make objects that appear more directly and more intimately to human experience.

Atsushi Maeda

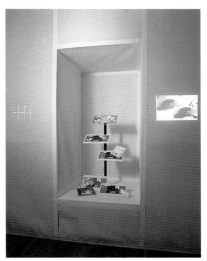

The Art of Ancient Mexico

DATE & LOCATION: 1992 September–December,
Haywood Gallery, London, England

TARGET AUDIENCE: General public

TYPE OF STAND: Temporary

SIZE (SQUARE METRES OR FEET): 1,300m

DESIGNER: Stanton Williams, London, England

STAND MANUFACTURER: Carlton Beck Ltd, England

CLIENT'S BRIEF: To exhibit the treasures of past
civilizations including Olmec, Aztec, Toltec and
Maya in the period 1000BC to 1500AD

DESIGN RATIONALE: The Exhibition was conceived as a
sequence of varying abstracted spaces with simple
dramatic architectural elements, a sloping floor in
the first gallery, a huge, angled wall in the second,
and a deep dividing wall with four large square
openings visually locking the spaces together,
acting as both window and showcase. Objects were
displayed at varying heights to emphasize scale and
distance. The lighting was designed to both create a
sense of isolation through individually spotlighting
objects and to accentuate the architectural
elements defining the spaces

Western Mexico

The Vital Gesture: Franz Kline in Retrospect

DATE & LOCATION: November 1985–March 1986, Cincinatti, Ohio, USA

TARGET AUDIENCE: General public

TYPE OF STAND: Temporary

SIZE (SQUARE METRES OR FEET): 930m

DESIGNER: Alan Baer, New York, USA

STAND MANUFACTURER: Patrick Eastlake

CLIENT'S BRIEF: Kline's paintings offer an encyclopedic range of concentrated expression based on human emotion and realised through muscular articulation of abstract form. Much of his most successful art generates strong physical sensations in the viewer yet subtleties of structure, light and atmosphere may not be readily perceived. A first rate Kline reveals its complexity and richness over time. An exhibition space had to be created to encompass the demands of this complex painter

DESIGN RATIONALE: The exhibition galleries were partitioned into smaller rooms to approximate the intimate scale of Kline's many studios and allowed for more wall space. As Kline preferred to paint at night, walls deepen in blue/black colour as one progressed through the exhibition. The temporary wooden walls were braced by cross beams and acknowledged the structuralist associations of Kline's paintings

ARCHITECT: Carl A. Strauss & Associates

EXHIBITION CO-ORDINATOR: Denny T. Young

FUNDING: Central Trust Company, National Endowment for the Arts and A.M. Kinney Inc.

GRAPHIC DESIGNER: Colophon

GUEST CURATOR: Harry F. Gough

PHOTOGRAPHY: Ron Forth

Figural Abstraction

Galleries devoted to the Arts of Africa and the Americas

DATE & LOCATION: Completed October 1987, Ohio, USA

TARGET AUDIENCE: General public

TYPE OF STAND: Permanent

SIZE (SQUARE METRES OR FEET): 280m

DESIGNER: Alan Baer, New York, USA

CLIENT'S BRIEF: To design a space to house life-size replicas of African villages and artefacts pertaining to everyday life

DESIGN RATIONALE: The galleries and cases within, represent a contextual response to a composite of environments where the displayed works were created and used. The cases contain references to native huts while the galleries suggest nature's encompassing omnipresence. Lush colour is employed to heighten the connection between the pieces being exhibited and their original settings

ARCHITECTS: Carl A. Strauss & Associates

Secret War

DATE & LOCATION: 1995 July, Imperial War Museum, London, England

TARGET AUDIENCE: General public

TYPE OF STAND: Permanent

SIZE (SQUARE METRES OR FEET): 3,200m

DESIGNER: James Dibble, Peter Higgins, Shirley Walker/Land Design Studio, London, England

STAND MANUFACTURER: Scena, England

CLIENT'S BRIEF: To recognise the importance of the history of clandestine warfare and at the same time, to address the question of its contemporary significance. To present a coherent storyline and relevant objects in a memorable and exciting way

DESIGN RATIONALE: The exhibition incorporates 3-D designs, sound, lighting, interactive video displays and graphic information to create a series of environmental narratives that allow the objects to be seen within different atmospheric contexts

AUDIOVISUAL: Spiral products

LIGHTING: Simon Tapping

PRODUCER: Sue Joly

SOUND: Julian Scott

intellektuell vorwegge
muß quasi wie der Kor
Werk realisieren, das
Phantasie der Archite
CAD, or computer-aid
and not drawing with
subsequently reducin
thinking up numerous
together, i.e. looking
aspect, in order to sel
computer, particu
visualise, qualify a
head of the design
It must never b
artistic or crea
nitely hard-working an
degree of freed
It does not pro
the designer has
in a matter of
the precision of th
design stage
es and produce
words and num
a piece of wo
the creative fa
brain, with
CAD, computer-aided-
ordinateu
commencer par
les angles possit
qualifier et de quantifie
par le cerveau du créat
des architectes de
Software

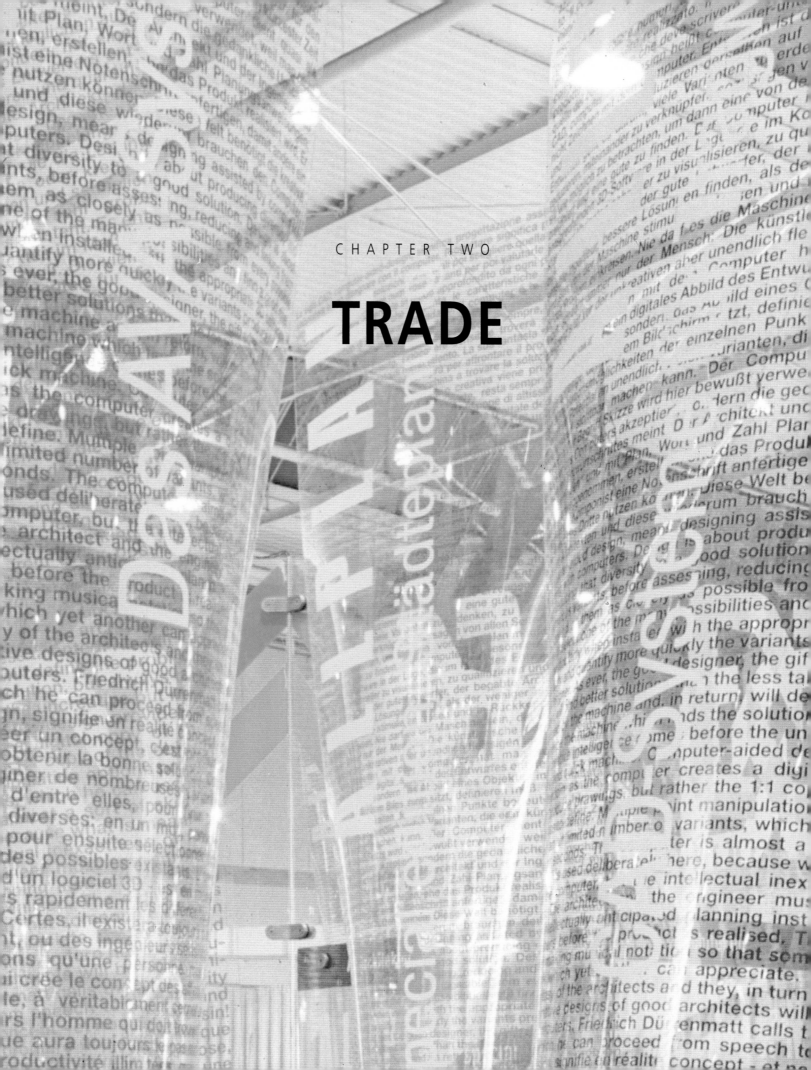

CHAPTER TWO

TRADE

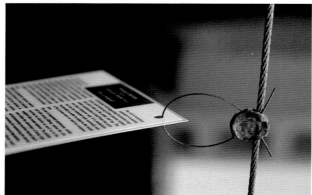

Fragile: Espace jeunes créateurs/Design, miroir du siècle/IKEA

DATE & LOCATION: 1993 July, Grand Palais, Paris, France

TARGET AUDIENCE: General Public, designers

TYPE OF STAND: One-off

SIZE (SQUARE METRES OR FEET): 240m

DESIGNER: Pippo Lionni & Associates, Paris, France

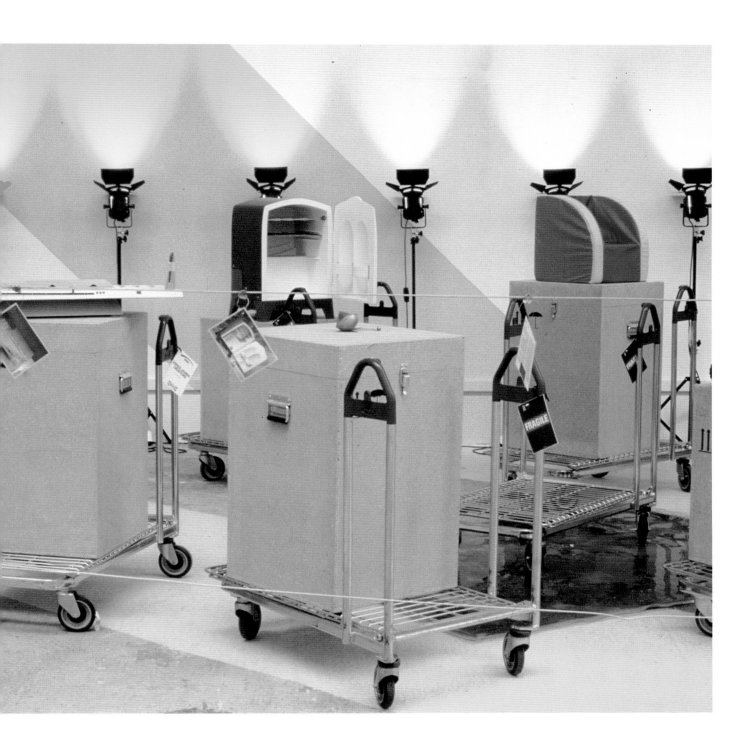

CLIENT'S BRIEF: To incorporate the idea of looking to the future from the other side of a mirror.
To design scenography and graphic communication for the presenting of young designers' work which expresses itself in all objects and sectors of everyday life

DESIGN RATIONALE: Luggage trolleys with cardboard boxes provided the base on which the exhibits were displayed. Each trolley had a tag with the lettering 'Fragile' on it to reiterate the overall message; "the meeting between the spectator and the spectated

in the same questioning discovery of the content - isolated and ever so fragile!" (preface of the exhibition catalogue)
PHOTOGRAPHER: Olivier Cadouin

Porca Miseria! - Light in the Tunnel

DATE & LOCATION: 1995 January, Cologne, Germany

TARGET AUDIENCE: Retailers, private clients

TYPE OF STAND: One-off

SIZE (SQUARE METRES OR FEET): Approximately 160m

DESIGNER: Ingo Maurer, Ingo Maurer GmbH, Munich, Germany

STAND MANUFACTURER: Ingo Maurer GmbH, Munich, Germany

CLIENT'S BRIEF: To create a daring, provocative and innovative stand in an unpretentious venue with a Bohemian flair to contrast with the prevailing mood of conservatism. To avoid repetition and reactionary nostalgia

DESIGN RATIONALE: A combination of light and movement created a poetic and playful work. Several thousand silver-coated leaves of varying sizes were mounted on thin metal rods. These were attached to a 'cloud' of metal gauze containing the light source and a fan ruffled the leaves. An aura of magic and mystery was created

PHOTOGRAPHER: Friedrich Busam

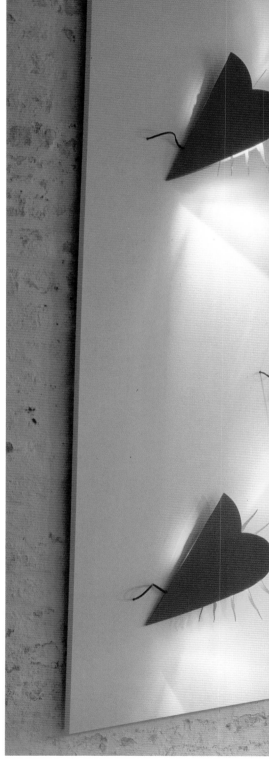

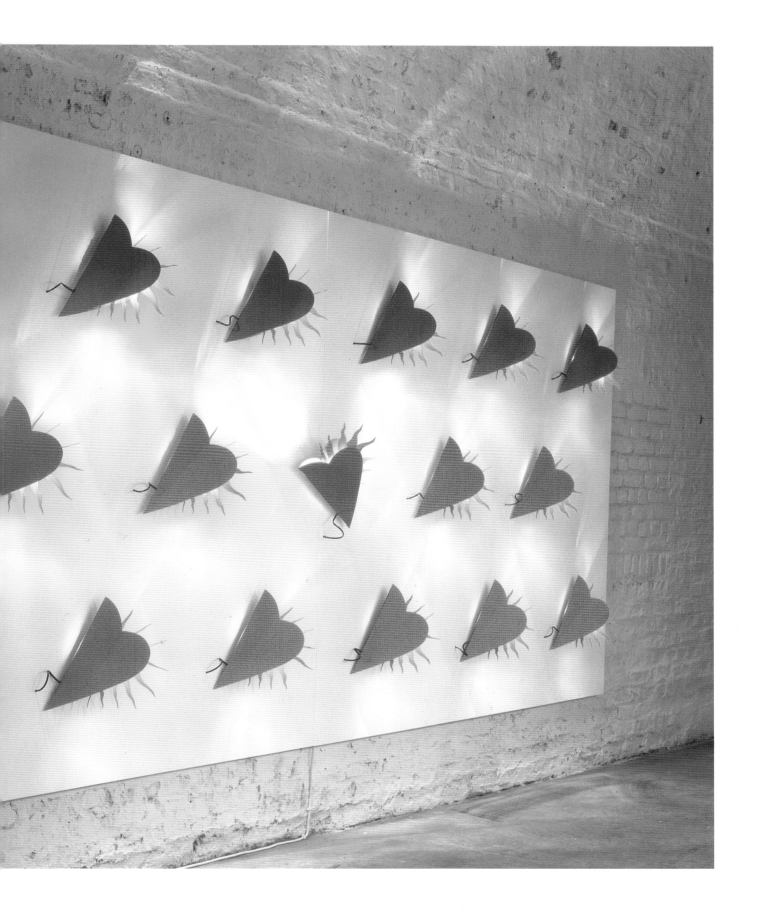

Computer Cab/Taxi Driver of the Year

DATE & LOCATION: 1994 August, Business Design Centre, London, England

TARGET AUDIENCE: General public (taxi drivers and their families)

TYPE OF STAND: One-off

SIZE (SQUARE METRES OR FEET): 150m

DESIGNER: Colin Sands, Terry Trickett/Trickett & Associates, London, England

CLIENT'S BRIEF: To demonstrate the benefits that Computer Cab offers drivers and its success in gaining large corporate customers

DESIGN RATIONALE: The Taxi Driver of the Year Show is a fun day out for the family. The giant letters TAXI are displayed in an entertaining way but also contain a serious message for drivers considering joining Computer Cab's fleet

PHOTOGRAPHER: Ian McKinnell

Sony Broadcast & Professionals Europe/International Broadcasting Convention

DATE & LOCATION: 1994 September, RAI Centre, Amsterdam, The Netherlands

TARGET AUDIENCE: Broadcast industry executives, personnel

TYPE OF STAND: One-off

SIZE (SQUARE METRES OR FEET): 1,000m

DESIGNER: Michael Littlechild/2LK Design, Farnham, England

CLIENT'S BRIEF: To design a stand confirming Sony's position as the industry leader. To communicate Sony's new age technology

DESIGN RATIONALE: Predominantly white structures with curves provided continuity. Co-ordinated graphics comprising simple strong shapes at low level, simple signage at eye level and suspended 12m high vertical signage for each product area were used to project sony's imposing position in the market place

PHOTOGRAPHER: Nicholas Gentilli & Associates

Nemetschek Programmsystem GmbH/Cebit '95

DATE & LOCATION: 1995 March, Hannover, Germany

TARGET AUDIENCE: Trade, architects, building engineers and property developers

TYPE OF STAND: One-off

SIZE (SQUARE METRES OR FEET): 132m

DESIGNER: Peter Hübner/Formpur, Riederich, Germany

STAND MANUFACTURER: Fairpur Messebau GmbH, Germany

CLIENT'S BRIEF: To create a stand that reflected the minimalist and modern image of the CAD and CAE software industry

DESIGN RATIONALE: The materials used to construct the stand and the equipment displayed has been allocated a specific place according to its function yet the mood is friendly not clinical and reflects the firm's philosophy: 'Planning is Everything'. Using transparent hangings which reflected the lights and movement of the screens a light, clean and sophisticated stand was designed

Astra/Cable & Satellite '95

DATE & LOCATION:1995 April, Olympia, London, England

TARGET AUDIENCE: Trade

TYPE OF STAND: One-off

SIZE (SQUARE METRES OR FEET): 176m

DESIGNER: Jeff Kindleysides/Checkland Kindleysides,
Leicester, England

CLIENT'S BRIEF: To portray Astra as the premier choice
for european satellite systems and demonstrate that
it is a rapidly expanding company at the forefront
of technological development in the distribution
and reception of television and radio broadcasts

DESIGN RATIONALE: A high-tech image was presented
through the use of clean, modern materials with
bold graphics creating an understanding of the
technology. Astra's central 'eye' feature
incorporated 64 live TV channels. The stand was
designed as a double deck to include a hospitality
area and optimise the use of available space

Iomega Booth/Comdex '94

DATE & LOCATION: Comdex '94, Las Vegas, USA

TARGET AUDIENCE: Computer trade

TYPE OF STAND: One-off

SIZE (SQUARE METRES OR FEET): 218m

DESIGNER: Jaimie Alexander, Alycia Freeman, Jonie Hupp, Paul Lechleiter, Paul Lycett, Sandy McKissick, Sarah Spatt, Eric Weissinger, Sheri Worrall/Fitch Inc, London, England

CLIENT'S BRIEF: To refect a new Iomega positioning. To show the variety and breadth of their products. To educate and inform their customers

DESIGN RATIONALE: A modern, experimental and flexible stand was created, eye-catching in its use of light and reflective materials. The booth had a strong educational and interactive thrust

IBM

DATE & LOCATION: 1994 March, National Exhibition Centre, Birmingham, England

TARGET AUDIENCE: Influential end-users

TYPE OF STAND: One-off

SIZE (SQUARE METRES OR FEET): Nine stands: 100-500m

DESIGNER: Innervisions Interiors & Exhibitions Ltd, London, England

CLIENT'S BRIEF: To design and project manage all aspects of IBM's new image as a vital entrepreneurial customer-centred organisation. To include key elements; enjoyment, surprise and openness

DESIGN RATIONALE: The nine individual stands served as the hubs for IBM 'villages' of dealers and associates. A series of dramatic fin shapes and a curved ceiling created a varied yet unified image across the stands. The lighting system enhanced the colour scheme

Monotype Systems Limited

DATE AND LOCATION: IPEX '93, National Exhibition Centre, Birmingham, England

PERMANENT, TRAVELLING OR ONE-OFF: One-off

SIZE (SQUARE METRES OR FEET): 250 Square metres

DESIGNER: Innervisions Interiors & Exhibitions Limited, London, England

TARGET AUDIENCE: Trade

CLIENT'S BRIEF: To show the full range of Monotype printing products divided by business units under the overall Monotype Systems brand

DESIGN RATIONALE: A series of dramatic, free flowing islands that provided an overall brand message together with individual sub-branding for the product and business units. The second level offered a combined group hospitality area. The stand also featured a "Then & Now" historical feature

(opposite page)

Monotype Systems

Herman Miller/Orgatec '94

DATE &LOCATION: 1994 Orgatec, Cologne, Germany

TARGET AUDIENCE: Office furniture buyers

TYPE OF STAND: One-off

SIZE (SQUARE METRES OR FEET): 100-300m

DESIGNER: BRS Premsela Vonk, Amsterdam, The Netherlands

CLIENT'S BRIEF: To introduce a new chair based on an entirely new ergonomic concept

DESIGN RATIONALE: The stand was divided by translucent partitions on which images, relating to the philosophy of the company, were projected. To create an ambient atmosphere, a high level of lighting was required and a strategic use of light sources enabled images to be projected

AGI Exhibition/AGI

DATE & LOCATION: 1994 March, san Jose, California, USA

TARGET AUDIENCE: Computer buyers

TYPE OF STAND: One-off

SIZE (SQUARE METRES OR FEET): 200ft

DESIGNER: Cliff Chung, John Hornall/Hornall Anderson,
Seattle, Washington, USA

STAND MANUFACTURER: Promotion Products Inc, USA

CLIENT'S BRIEF: To demonstrate the wide range of
packaging that AGI print

DESIGN RATIONALE: The zig-zag design used reflected
the diverse range of printing products. The design
mirrored the high-tech approach adopted by the
company

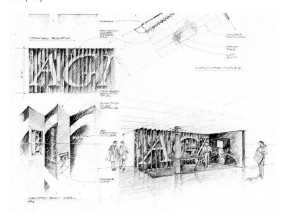

Phonehouse/Direct Line Insurance plc

DATE & LOCATION: 1995 March, Earl's Court, London, England

TARGET AUDIENCE: General public, 18 years and over

TYPE OF STAND: One-off

SIZE (SQUARE METRES OR FEET): 45m

DESIGNER: Northcross, London, England

CLIENT'S BRIEF: To create a powerful promotional tool which built on Direct Line's strong identity

DESIGN RATIONALE: Sculptors worked with polystyrene to create a 22ft high model this was then plastered in preparation for moulds to be made. In total 26 sections of moulded, painted and polished fibreglass were bolted together. Within the house, multi-level presentations and viewing galleries, were provided in the mouth and the ear pieces. Information was imparted using video screens, light and sound effects and interactive product displays

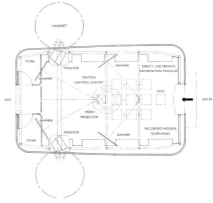

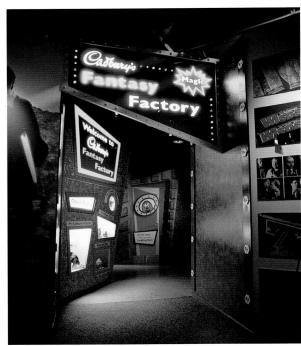

Fantasy Factory/
Cadbury Ltd

DATE & LOCATION: 1994 April, Cadbury World,
Bournville, Birmingham, England

TARGET AUDIENCE: 4-10 year olds

TYPE OF STAND: Permanent

SIZE (SQUARE METRES OR FEET): Approximately 350m

DESIGNER: Lynne Boon/Imagination, London, England

CLIENT'S BRIEF: To create a Cadbury World leisure
attraction for children whilst including Cadbury's
corporate values of quality and dedication in an
unobtrusive yet totally focused fashion

DESIGN RATIONALE: A hands-on experience was created
meeting children's high expectations for a fun-filled
play area

ART DIRECTOR: Nick Fraser

LIGHTING: Jonathan Howard

Philips Electronics/Live '94

DATE & LOCATION: 1994 September, London, England

TARGET AUDIENCE: Trade and males 16-35 years

TYPE OF STAND: One-off

SIZE (SQUARE METRES OR FEET): 580m

DESIGNER: Innervisions Interiors & Exhibitions Ltd, London, England

CLIENT'S BRIEF: To create a lively, bold environment to display a range of consumer electronic products (TV, CDI, DCC, Satellite products)

DESIGN RATIONALE: Fabric flutes projected changing images of current titles onto circular canopies. The flutes were lit in a variety of strong colours, creating an attractive, fluid display

PHILIPS
CRYSTALCLEAR
PHILIPS
100 Hertz · · Widescreen
Portables · · · · · Portables · · · · Mono fst · · · · · Nicam

Svoboda/Orgatec '94

DATE & LOCATION: 1994 October, Cologne, Germany

TARGET AUDIENCE: Corporate community and office managers

TYPE OF STAND: Temporary

SIZE (SQUARE METRES OR FEET): 180m

STAND MAUFACTURER: Svoboda Buromobel, Germany

DESIGNER: Nick Butcher, Christian Davies/Fitch, London, England

CLIENT'S BRIEF: To communicate Svoboda's brand value and philosophy in conjunction with the launch of 'SEO'; a range of executive furniture. To create a niche for Svoboda in the German office marketplace

DESIGN RATIONALE: A wooden path led the audience through areas of subtle lighting which contained Svoboda's furniture. The lighting was diffused by the striking yet warm colours of the display panels to create an atmosphere of professionalism and familiarity

PHOTOGRAPHER: Jon O'Brien

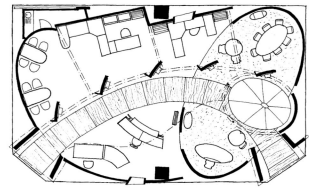

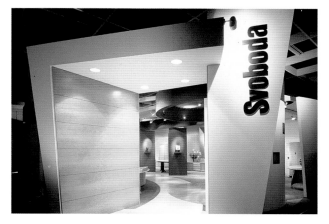

Microsoft/Windows '95

DATE & LOCATION: 1995 February-March, London, England

TARGET AUDIENCE: Influential end-users

TYPE OF STAND: Temporary

SIZE (SQUARE METRES OR FEET): 550m

DESIGNER: Innervisions Interiors & Exhibitions Ltd

CLIENT'S BRIEF: To create a platform for Microsoft's products and applications. To provide a dramatic theatrical environment for a preview of a Microsoft vision of the future whilst ensuring a maximum audience interest

DESIGN RATIONALE: A series of open theatres and hands-on test drives focused around a 12m high circular tower which contained a spectacular interactive presentation. This featured 140 monitors, drop screens and pre-programmed light and laser show

Intel (Europe) GmbH/CeBit '93

DATE & LOCATION: 1993 March, Hanover, Germany

TARGET AUDIENCE: General public

TYPE OF STAND: One-off

SIZE (SQUARE METRES OR FEET): 1,000m

DESIGNER: Innervisions Interiors & Exhibitions Ltd, London, England

CLIENT'S BRIEF: To strengthen the Intel brand, show a range of current and future technologies in an innovative way to the visiting public whilst providing a serious business environment. To provide an arena for Intel's new Pentium processor

DESIGN RATIONALE: Themed stage areas showed the new technologies with short, humourous plays. Placing the products as part of everyday life, two-tiered computer stations were purpose-built for hands on demonstrations

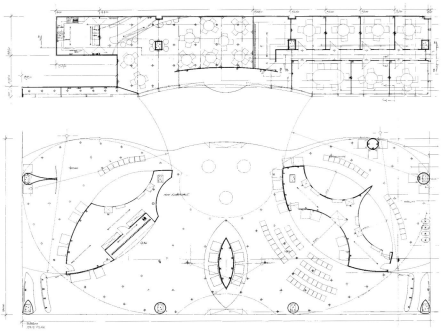

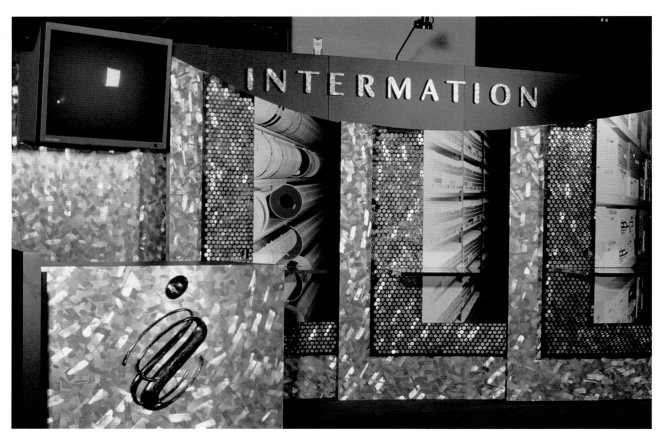

Intermation/Corporation Intermation Exhibition

DATE & LOCATION: 1993 September, Seattle, Washington, USA

TARGET AUDIENCE: Corporate buyers

TYPE OF STAND: One-off

SIZE (SQUARE METRES OR FEET): 150ft

DESIGNER: Jack Anderson, Cliff Chung/Hornall Anderson, Seattle, Washington, USA

STAND MANUFACTURER: Turner Exhibits, USA

CLIENT'S BRIEF: To design a high-tech, state of the art display for their products

DESIGN RATIONALE: A wafer-board texture finish on aluminium was used with heat treated, perforated panels. The focus was on Duo-tone photographs representing the different storage capabilities

ART DIRECTOR: Jack Anderson

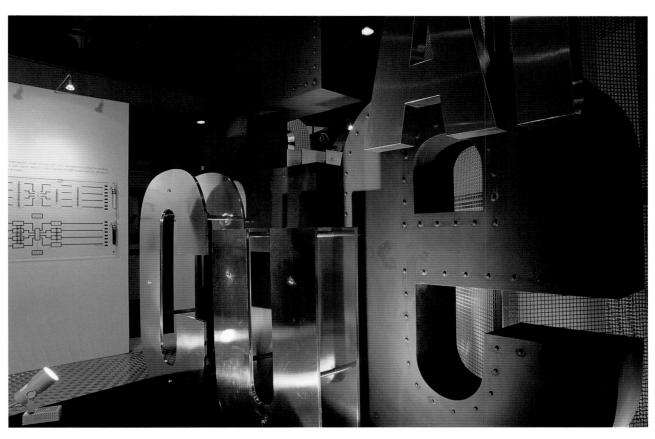

Kuwait Petroleum Lubricants/Mach '92

DATE & LOCATION: 1992 March, National Exhibition Centre, Birmingham, England

TARGET AUDIENCE: Engineers, specifiers of metal cutting lubricants

TYPE OF STAND: One-off

SIZE (SQUARE METRES OR FEET): 96m

DESIGNER: Terry Grant, Neil Smith/Giant, London, England

STAND MANUFACTURER: Decor and Display Ltd, England

CLIENT'S BRIEF: To create a striking stand, to launch Kuwait Petroleum Lubricant's range of metalworking lubricants to the industrial market

DESIGN RATIONALE: The floor plan was based on the curves within the Q8 logo which were echoed by the display screens. A centrepiece was designed which featured an arrangement of chemical symbols constructed from the appropriate metals

Apple Computer/
Apple Expo '94

DATE & LOCATION: 1994 October, Olympia, London, England

TARGET AUDIENCE: Trade

TYPE OF STAND: One-off

SIZE (SQUARE METRES OR FEET): 300m

DESIGNER: Innervisions Interiors & Exhibitions Ltd, London, England

CLIENT'S BRIEF: To design the hub of the annual Apple Expo Show. To display the whole range of Apple's hardware products and software applications

DESIGN RATIONALE: The various products and applications were arranged around a series of illuminated gondolas. Extensive use was made of theatrical lighting effects playing on a dramatically suspended ceiling structure, visible from all angles

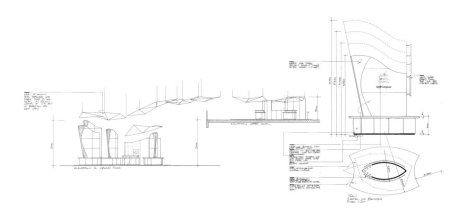

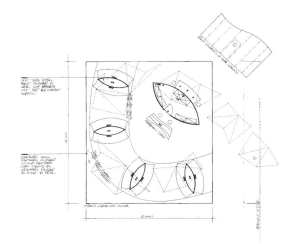

JBL/Live '94

DATE & LOCATION: 1994, London, England

TARGET AUDIENCE: UK consumers

TYPE OF STAND: One-off

SIZE (SQUARE METRES OR FEET): Approximately 86m

STAND MANUFACTURER: Twenty First Century Exhibitions, England

DESIGNER: Jane Brady, Stephen Burks, Christie Koehler, Mike Mooney, Kate Murphy/Fitch Inc, Boston, USA

CLIENT'S BRIEF: To display their new product lines to the UK using an existing mini-theatre, a power packed mini-van and four diverse retail displays

DESIGN RATIONALE: The three existing elements were interlinked to create a coherent consumer presentation. The stand acted as a backdrop for the mini-theatre, circulation was simplified.
A concentrated visual presentation of the global brand was created

Storage Works/CEBIT '94

DATE & LOCATION: 1994, Hanover, Germany

TARGET AUDIENCE: Information specialists

TYPE OF STAND: One-off

SIZE (SQUARE METRES OR FEET): 300m

DESIGNER: Furneaux Stewart, London, England

CLIENT'S BRIEF: To provide a memorable and dramatic stand for the digital company Storage Works

DESIGN RATIONALE: The focal point of the stand was the conical, oval tower, rising 6 metres providing an umbrella for various bars, meeting rooms, product areas and a live action stage. A series of continual moving images were projected onto the tensile cone to create changing moods

MET Studio/
Cruise and Ferry '95

DATE & LOCATION: 1995 May, Olympia, London, England

TARGET AUDIENCE: Trade

TYPE OF STAND: One-off

SIZE (SQUARE METRES OR FEET): 16m

DESIGNER: Sian Hooper/MET Studio Ltd, London, England

STAND MANUFACTURER: Carlton Beck, England

CLIENT'S BRIEF: To illustrate MET Studio's work in both the museum and leisure fields

DESIGN RATIONALE: The letters M E T were the focal point, the 'M' stood at 4m high, on the reverse were images reflecting the diversity of their work. The 'T' was used to store promotional material. The stand included a tensile sail-like structure, a model and framed prints from the Queen Elizabeth II refurbishment project (1994). Post cards on the front of the 'M' reflected the international nature of MET Studio's work

PHOTOGRAPHER: Chris Hollick

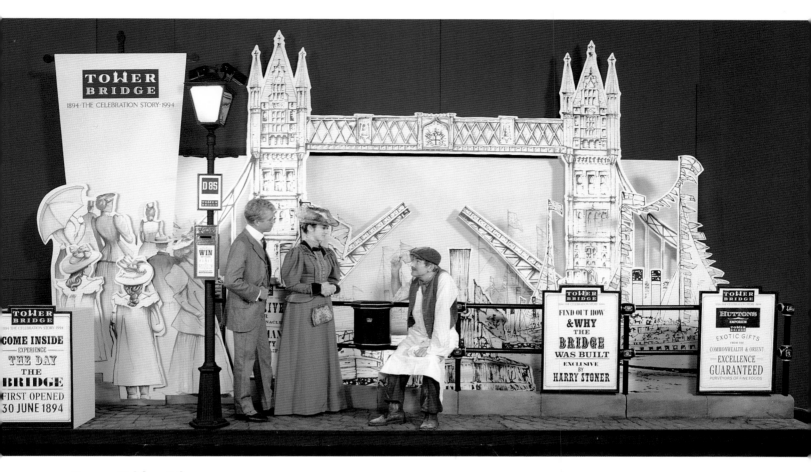

Tower Bridge 'The Celebration Story'/World Travel Market

DATE &LOCATION: 1993, World Travel Market, Olympia, London, England

TARGET AUDIENCE: Travel trade

TYPE OF STAND: One-off

SIZE (SQUARE METRES OR FEET): 32m

DESIGNER: Ian Kenny/Conceptor International, London, England

STAND MANUFACTURER: Terance Dickson Associates

CLIENT'S BRIEF: To present the Tower Bridge permanent exhibition prior to its completion without giving away detail but generating media and trade interest

DESIGN RATIONALE: The focus was on the bridge at its peak and its official opening, 30th June 1894. All aspects of the exhibit were displayed theatrically

Sony/Live '94

DATE & LOCATION: 1994 September, Earl's Court,
London, England

TARGET AUDIENCE: Consumer electronics

TYPE OF STAND: One-off

SIZE (SQUARE METRES OR FEET): 2,400m

DESIGNER: John Young/MICE Group, London, England

STAND MANUFACTURER: Silver Knight/Guiltspur, England

CLIENT'S BRIEF: To be shown as a complete
entertainment company from professional studio to
the home incorporating Columbia Pictures, Sony
music, data media and cutting edge technology, the
stand had to be fun, exciting and informative

DESIGN RATIONALE: The stand was designed on several
levels, a pedestrianised flyover led the visitor up a
gangway from a garden surrounded by railings to
the upper levels. A tunnel was illuminated with
repetitive images echoing the outside simulated
flyover

EVENT MANAGER: Mike MacLaghlan

Reuters/Forex '94

DATE & LOCATION: 1994, London, England

TARGET AUDIENCE: Forex dealers

TYPE OF STAND: One-off

SIZE (SQUARE METRES OR FEET): 200m

DESIGNER: Innervisions Interiors & Exhibitions Ltd, London, England

CLIENT'S BRIEF: To create an eye-catching, futuristic exhibit to position Reuters firmly as the market leader in the Forex arena. To display new technology such as Dealing 2000 with an 'attract' feature

DESIGN RATIONALE: The stand featured an enclosed interactive theatre located on the ground floor of the stand. An elevated walkway was lined with hands-on demonstrations of Reuters products, set within a dramatic, futuristic architecture of metal, glass and fabric

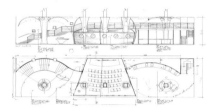

BT/Innovation '94

DATE &LOCATION: 1994 March, Martlesham, Suffolk, England

TARGET AUDIENCE: Chief executives

TYPE OF STAND: One-off

SIZE (SQUARE METRES OR FEET): 1,315m

DESIGNER: Imagination, London, England

CLIENT'S BRIEF: To demystify the hype surrounding multimedia and video-on-demand. To create a piece of effective communication to bring BT's research and development to life for key strategic business partners

DESIGN RATIONALE: A fully enclosed 'Black Box' of nine themed areas provided a completely immersing walk-through experience. BT's own scientists were coached to take visitors through particular technological developments

Acclaim Entertainment Ltd/Future Entertainment

DATE & LOCATION: 1993 September, Earl's Court, London, England

TARGET AUDIENCE: Teenagers

TYPE OF STAND: One-off

SIZE (SQUARE METRES OR FEET): 250m

DESIGNER: Innervisions Interiors & Exhibitions Ltd, London, England

CLIENT'S BRIEF: To generate excitement for the forthcoming season's computer games products and to provide a 'hands-on' game forum for Acclaim's audience

DESIGN RATIONALE: A 'Street Talk' show theme was developed. This naturally led to the tailoring of the stand in the style of a New York Street Scene, featuring large scale murals, graffiti art and a real Checker cab

Compaq Computer Network '94

DATE & LOCATION: 1994 June, National Exhibition Centre, Birmingham, England

TARGET AUDIENCE: Telecom managers

TYPE OF STAND: One-off

SIZE (SQUARE METRES OR FEET): 300m

DESIGNER: Innervisions Interiors & Exhibitions Ltd, London, England

CLIENT'S BRIEF: To clearly separate Compaq's products into different market segments and to allow maximum flow and visibility across the stand

DESIGN RATIONALE: A series of open framed metalwork islands were constructed around a central hub. Each island was dramatically lit by theatrical lighting

HBJ Treasury of Literature Exhibit

DATE & LOCATION: 1992 May, Orlando, Florida

TARGET AUDIENCE: Teaching profession

TYPE OF STAND: One-off

DESIGNER: Kent Hunter, Jeff Jordan, David Suh/Frankfurt Balkind Partners, New York, USA

CLIENT'S BRIEF: To generate awareness of the new reading programme, prior to and during product sampling, to differentiate the product from the competitors' to establish the 'Treasury of Literature' programme as the gold standard

DESIGN RATIONALE: A broad range of colours and graphics were used to make the stand easily accessible to the viewer. A yellow brick road guided the visitor through the exhibit with messages reinforcing the importance of reading

BTicino

DATE & LOCATION: 1995, Lighting Exhibition, Milan, Italy

TARGET AUDIENCE: Trade

TYPE OF STAND: One-off

SIZE (SQUARE METRES OR FEET): 256m

DESIGNER: Italo Lupi, Milan, Italy

CLIENT'S BRIEF: To promote BT icino's products and present two new series of electric switches

DESIGN RATIONALE: The four walls of the central hall were painted yellow, blue, red and green providing the backdrops for striking three-dimensional graphics

Ahrend Group/Orgatec '94

DATE & LOCATION: 1994 October, Orgatec '94, Cologne, Germany

TARGET AUDIENCE: Office furniture buyers, interior designers and architects

TYPE OF STAND: One-off

SIZE (SQUARE METRES OR FEET): 200m

DESIGNER: Radboud van Beekum, Total Design Amsterdam bv, The Netherlands

STAND MANUFACTURER: Ahrend Service Group, The Netherlands

CLIENT'S BRIEF: To provide information about three existing and three new product groups using a simple arrangement of the products to create a warm ambience

DESIGN RATIONALE: A marketsquare atmosphere was created where products were displayed and offered for sale. A framework made from wooden rafters and canvas towered above the stand to serve as a ceiling and wall

LIGHTING CONSULTANTS: Hans Wolff & Partners, Amsterdam, The Netherlands

PHOTOGRAPHER: Roos Aldershoff, Amsterdam, The Netherlands

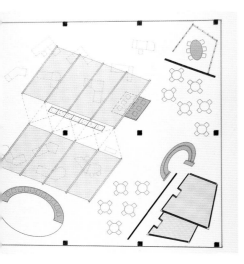

Citroën/Salon International de L'Automobile

DATE & LOCATION: 1995 March, Geneva, Switzerland

TARGET AUDIENCE: General public

TYPE OF STAND: One-off

SIZE (SQUARE METRES OR FEET): Approximately 1,200m

DESIGNER: Arnaud Saillan/HG Créations, Boulogne, France

CLIENT'S BRIEF: To build a stand to demonstrate Citroën's committment to their new slogan. To reflect the Xanae's exciting new identity whilst maintaining Citroën's established values

DESIGN RATIONALE: A welcoming environment was created by displaying the car on a central podium, a dance show was performed around the vehicle. Fluid and undulating forms, warm and natural materials and clear colours were selected and enhanced by the lighting

CHOREOGRAPHER: Laurie Moerman/Blue Vision

GRAPHIC DESIGNER: Pierre Vrai/Saalchli

LIGHTING TECHNICIAN: Eric Lherminier/ Référénce

PHOTOGRAPHER: Thierry Biaujeaud/Bleue Image

STYLIST: Sophie Saidi/Blue Vision

Citroën Ulster Show Stand

DATE & LOCATION: 1994 February, Ulster, Belfast, Ireland

TARGET AUDIENCE: General public, fleet buyers

TYPE OF STAND: One-off

SIZE (SQUARE METRES OR FEET): 600m

DESIGNER: Furneaux Stewart, London, England

STAND MANUFACTURER: Plus 2, Architen, Helm Exhibitions, England

CLIENT'S BRIEF: To maximise long distance views and branding opportunities in a highly competitve trade show environment

DESIGN RATIONALE: High tensile structures were used to compliment Citroën's sponsorship of gliding and yachting events. A visual link combined these shapes with the purity of the tensiles to provide a dramatic setting for the launch of the new Citroën ZX Estate

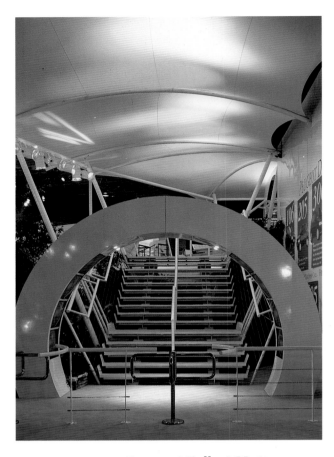

Peugeot Talbot Motor Company/International Motorshow '94

DATE & LOCATION: 1994 October, Birmingham, England

TARGET AUDIENCE: Consumer, trade

TYPE OF STAND: One-off

SIZE (SQUARE METRES OR FEET): 2,100m

DESIGNER: Innervisions Interiors & Exhibitions Ltd, London, England

CLIENT'S BRIEF: To show Peugeot's entire range of cars and commercial vehicles. To launch Peugeot's participation in Formula One racing and to educate the public on the benefits of diesel

DESIGN RATIONALE: The exhibition was held on two adjacent sites. The main structure linked both sites over the public gangway, integrating a main walkway as part of the exhibit. It featured models, diagrams and interactive displays

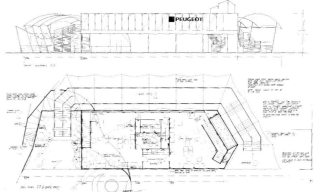

Mazda Stand

DATE & LOCATION: 1994 October, National Exhibition Centre, Birmingham, England

TARGET AUDIENCE: Trade

TYPE OF STAND: One-off

SIZE (SQUARE METRES OR FEET): 1,006m

DESIGNER: Harper Mackay Ltd, London, England

STAND MANUFACTURER: Harper Mackay Productions Ltd, London, England

CLIENT'S BRIEF: To promote the sensuous nature of their product. To create a 'Mazda' environment clear of the detritus of the general ambience around

DESIGN RATIONALE: This was achieved by a controlling ground plane and floating roof plane

Porsche Motorshow Stand

DATE & LOCATION: 1993 October, Earl's Court, London, England

TARGET AUDIENCE: General public, motor specialists

TYPE OF STAND: One-off

SIZE (SQUARE METRES OR FEET): 450m

DESIGNER: Furneaux Stewart, London England

STAND MANUFACTURER: Early Action Group, Helm Exhibitions, England

CLIENT'S BRIEF: To celebrate thirty years of the Porsche 911 design evolution

DESIGN RATIONALE: Cars from each decade were displayed on a banked circuit wall. Continuous history plinths at the foot of the wall carried texts. These showed world events accompanied by the specific 911 model developments

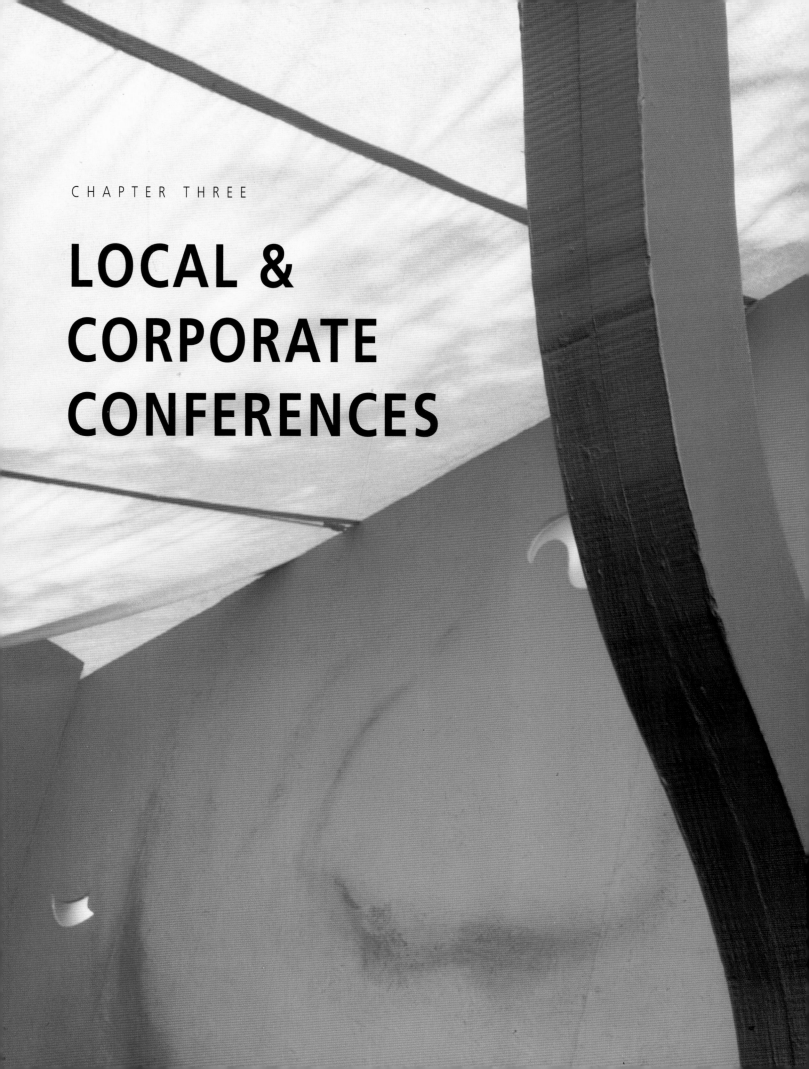

CHAPTER THREE

LOCAL & CORPORATE CONFERENCES

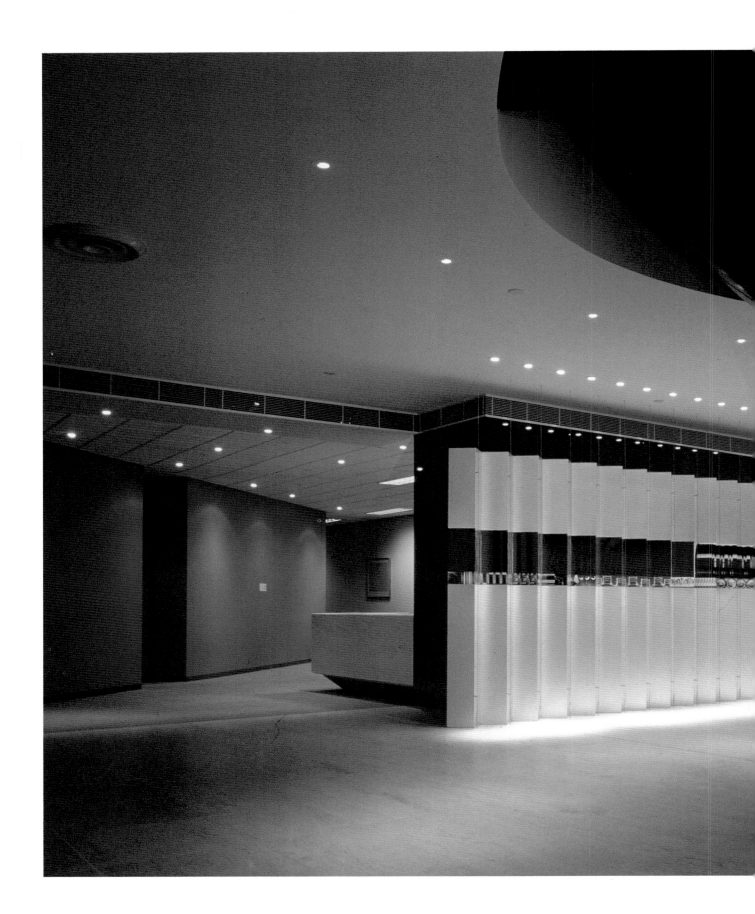

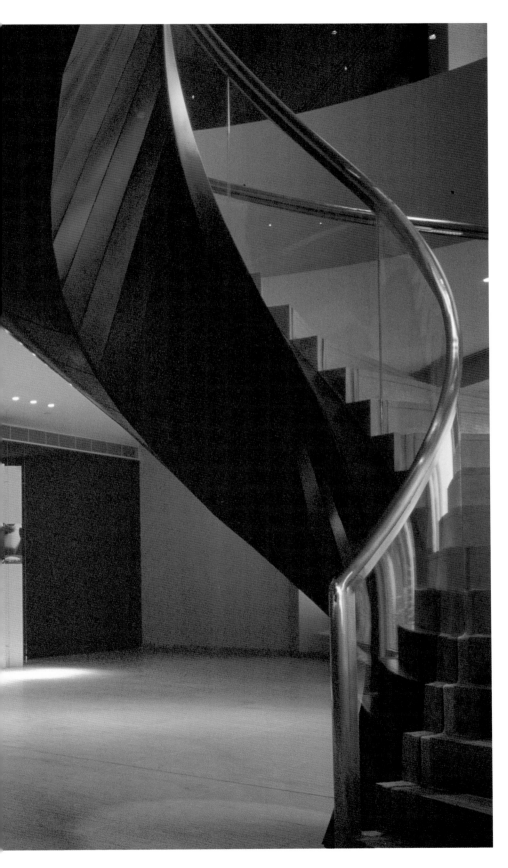

Amcor Ltd

DATE & LOCATION: 1993, Head Office Foyer, Melbourne, Australia

TARGET AUDIENCE: The Corporate community

TYPE OF STAND: Permanent

DESIGNER: Garry Emery/Emery Vincent Design, South Melbourne, Victoria, Australia

STAND MANUFACTURER: Consolidated Graphics, Australia

CLIENT'S BRIEF: To convey an impression of the company, past and present and it's products

DESIGN RATIONALE: Viewed from one direction the display shows historic information, from the other the company as it is today

(continued from 144–5, Amcor Ltd, Melbourne, Australia)

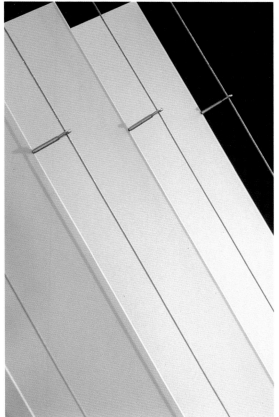

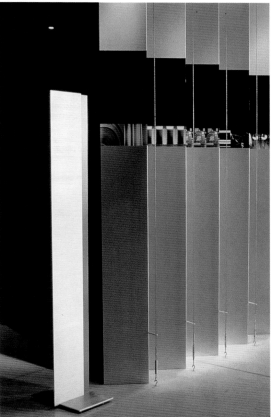

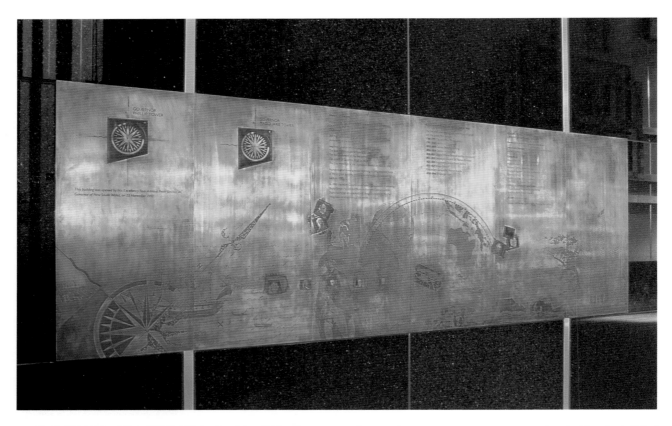

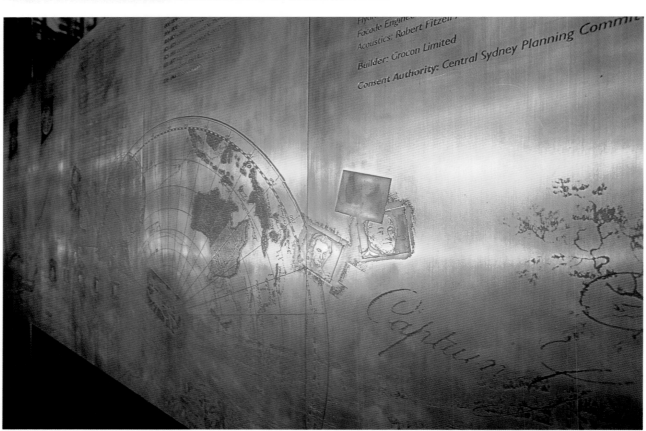

Governor Phillip Tower

DATE & LOCATION: 1994, Governor Phillip Tower foyer,
Sydney, Australia

TARGET AUDIENCE: Corporate community

TYPE OF STAND: Permanent

DESIGNER: Garry Emery/Emery Vincent Design, South
Melbourne, Victoria, Australia

CLIENT'S BRIEF: To develop a system of display panels
conveying information about the historic nature of
the building site whilst being appropriate to the
contemporary architectural design of the building

DESIGN RATIONALE: The design solution utilises historic
imagery interpreted in a contemporary context. The
images are acid etched in multiple layers into sheet
bronze and stainless steel

Argento è Luce

DATE & LOCATION: 1994, Gallerie Sawaya & Moroni, Milan, Italy

TARGET AUDIENCE: General public

TYPE OF STAND: Temporary

DESIGNER: William Sawaya/Sawaya & Moroni, Milan, Italy

CLIENT'S BRIEF: To represent an eclectic collection of artefacts in a cohesive and intellectually stimulating way

DESIGN RATIONALE: Away from the enclosed environment of the gallery, the collection would normally have appeared at loggerheads with one another. In the gallery the materials and forms created an 'ambience delabrée'. The overall mood was literary and aimed to underline the importance of visual communication with the audience

The People's City

DATE & LOCATION: 1995 March-April, Barcelona, Spain

TARGET AUDIENCE: General public

TYPE OF STAND: One-off

SIZE (SQUARE METRES OR FEET): 1,000m

DESIGNER: Victor Vilaseca/Vilaseca & Altarriba Associats, Barcelona, Spain

STAND MANUFACTURER: J. C. Montiel, F. Marza, Spain

CLIENT'S BRIEF: To provide information on the Council's past, present and future projects in a clear and accessible way

DESIGN RATIONALE: Serigraphed paper was used as a background on which to display photographs and explanations. A virtual theatre was constructed, audiovisuals and self-learning systems were also installed

Philips Competence Centre

DATE & LOCATION: 1993 November, Eindhoven, The Netherlands

TARGET AUDIENCE: Corporate visitors, selected public groups

TYPE OF STAND: Permanent

SIZE (SQUARE METRES OR FEET): 4,000m

DESIGNER: Bruce Burdick, Susan K. Burdick/The Burdick Group. San Francisco, California, USA

STAND MANUFACTURER: Carlton Benbow Contracts, Devon, England, Gielissen bv, Eindhoven, The Netherlands

CLIENT'S BRIEF: To provide an overview of the total competency of their diverse product divisions

DESIGN RATIONALE: The existing dome structure was renovated as the front door of the centre. Theatre pavilions were built using steel, etched and clear glass and bead blasted aluminium. Around each level's perimeter a continuous glowing light wall provides colourful backdrop for the exhibits. Interactive displays, computer programmes and films were installed as part of the educative function

PHOTOGRAPHER: Herman de Winter, USA

Ring 3 - Professional Innovation Exhibits

Ring 2 - Consumer Innovation Exhibits

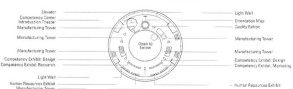

Ring 1 - Foundation Competency Exhibits

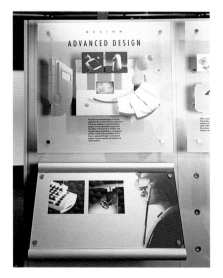

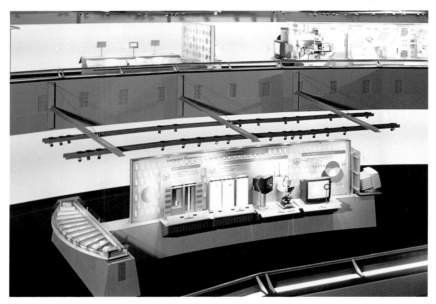

(continued from pp 154–5
Philips Competence Centre, Eindhoven,
The Netherlands)

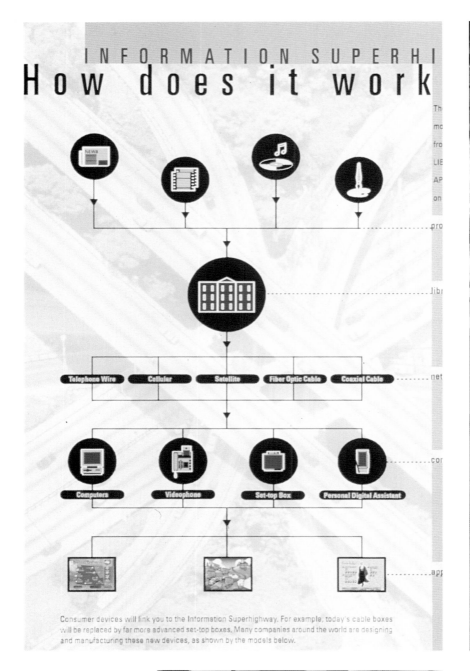

INFORMATION SUPERHI

How does it work

Telephone Wire | Cellular | Satellite | Fiber Optic Cable | Coaxial Cable

Computers | Videophone | Set-top Box | Personal Digital Assistant

Consumer devices will link you to the Information Superhighway. For example, today's cable boxes will be replaced by far more advanced set-top boxes. Many companies around the world are designing and manufacturing these new devices, as shown by the models below.

Information Superhighway Exhibit/Oracle Corporation

DATE: 1994 September

TARGET AUDIENCE: General public

TYPE OF STAND: Permanent

SIZE (SQUARE METRES OR FEET): 1,000ft

DESIGNER: Susan K. Burdick/The Burdick Group, San Francisco, California, USA

STAND MANUFACTURER: General Exhibits, Chicago, Illinois, USA

CLIENT'S BRIEF: To introduce visitors to the Information Superhighway and provide them with an idea of how it will effect their daily lives

DESIGN RATIONALE: The Information Superhighway is put into context for visitors through a central theatre area containing three video walls. Interactive stations allow visitors to test typical applications relating to entertainment, education and retail. A LED word-display attracts visitors by identifying the range of ways the Information Highway can be used

PHOTOGRAPHY: The Burdick Group

The Channel Islands: Occupation and Liberation, 1940–1945

DATE & LOCATION: 1995 April–1996 January, Imperial War Museum, London, England

TARGET AUDIENCE: General public

TYPE OF STAND: One-off

SIZE (SQUARE METRES OR FEET): 200m

DESIGNER: Charlotte Ross, Andrew Thomas, Terry Trickett, Lynn Trickett/Trickett Associates, London, England

CLIENT'S BRIEF: To mark the 50th anniversary of the Liberation of the Channel Islands. To explain why the islands were invaded in 1940 and how liberation came about in 1945. To convey what life was like under the occupying force and the different experiences of those who lived and died during it

DESIGN RATIONALE: The exhibition presents a series of 'scenes' which convey the sense of fear under which the islanders were forced to live for five long years. It provides a reminder that the islands still bear scars – in the form of vast concrete fortifications and in the less tangible form of personal experiences and memories

The Museum at Portland head

DATE & LOCATION: 1992 September, Fort Williams Park, Cape Elizabeth, Maine, USA

TARGET AUDIENCE: General public, tourists

TYPE OF STAND: Permanent

SIZE (SQUARE METRES OR FEET): 1,700ft

DESIGNER: Sam van Dam, Rick Renner, Brad Woodworth/Woodworth Associates, Portland, Maine, USA

STAND MANUFACTURER: F.W. Dixon & Co, USA

CLIENT'S BRIEF: To portray two centuries of social, economic, military and maritime history surrounding this famous landmark

DESIGN RATIONALE: Photographs, maps, models, artifacts and descriptive texts are used to relate the story of Portland Head Light from mariner's perspective

DESIGNER: David Adams

LIGHTING CONSULTANT: James Stockman

MODELMAKER: Craig Toftey

RESEARCHER: Christiane Mathan

WRITERS: Nancy Brooks, Melissa Kelly, Megan Thorn

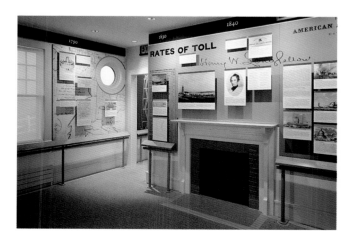

BT Goonhilly Visitor Centre

DATE & LOCATION: 1994 April, BT Goonhilly Earth Satellite Earth Station, Cornwall, England

TARGET AUDIENCE: General public

TYPE OF STAND: Permanent

SIZE (SQUARE METRES OR FEET): 200m

DESIGNER: Furneaux Stewart, London, England

STAND MANUFACTURER: Helm Exhibitions, Architen, BBA Graphics, England

CLIENT'S BRIEF: To educate visitors about the latest satellite communication systems and their many applications

DESIGN RATIONALE: A metal dome was constructed to create a 'visitor walk through journey' where graphics and video displays are set into real satellite-dish backdrops. Interactive displays were installed so that the visitor can learn about fax and videophone communication

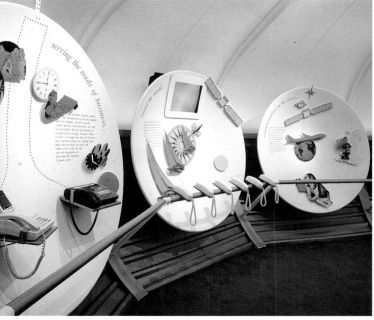

163

The Story of Popular Photography

DATE & LOCATION: 1989, National Museum of
Photography, Film & Television, Bradford, England

TARGET AUDIENCE: General public

TYPE OF STAND: Permanent

DESIGNER: In-house design team

CLIENT'S BRIEF: To illustrate that early Victorian
photography was a rich man's hobby

DESIGN RATIONALE: A Victorian parlour was re-created
using original antique furniture. This was modified
to make museum-quality showcases to display a
huge range of unique and valuable objects

Rochester Guild Hall Museum/Rochester-upon-Medway City Council

DATE & LOCATION: 1994, Rochester, Kent, England

TARGET AUDIENCE: General public

TYPE OF STAND: Permanent

SIZE (SQUARE METRES OR FEET): 500m over fourteen rooms

DESIGNER: Ronayne Design, London, England

CLIENT'S BRIEF: To illustrate local historical themes chronologically using the 17th century Guild Hall and the adjacent Edwardian building

DESIGN RATIONALE: A principal exhibit is the recreated-creation, on three levels, of a convict ship. Mirrored walls are used to expand the size of gallery rooms. Interactive displays allow visitors to mint a coin, take an impression of the city seal, load a musket and view the city using a panoramic camera at roof top level

Enkhuizen
Historical Museum

DATE & LOCATION: Enkhuizen, The Netherlands

TARGET AUDIENCE: General public

TYPE OF STAND: Permanent

DESIGNER: René van Raalte/BRS Premsela Vonk, Amsterdam, The Netherlands

CLIENT'S BRIEF: To take visitors through the historic traditions of Enkhuizen's whaling industry

DESIGN RATIONALE: Part of a ship's hull and a merchant's house displayed items used in the whaling industry. A house constructed of old sails aimed to mirror the movement of the winds and arctic conditions found at the north pole. A smell of tar and blubber pervaded the exhibition to give an extra sense of realism

The Dockyard Apprentice

DATE & LOCATION: 1994 May, Portsmouth Historic
Dockyard, Portsmouth Naval Base Property Trust,
Portsmouth, England

TARGET AUDIENCE: General Public

TYPE OF STAND: Permanent

SIZE (SQUARE METRES OR FEET): 500m

DESIGNER: Ian Kenny, Sam Ross/Conceptor
International, London, England

STAND MANUFACTURER: Terance Dickson Associates

CLIENT'S BRIEF: To tell the story of life in the dockyard
and to explain the skills and technology utilised in
the ship building industry

DESIGN RATIONALE: The design uses life-size models in
period costumes demonstrating the various daily
tasks of the dockyard apprentice. Display panels
present detailed information on the various aspects
of shipping technology

ADDITIONAL CREDITS: Q.T.S, T.V.C, England

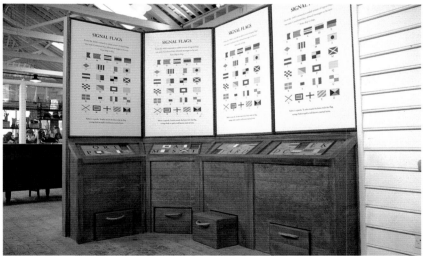

Collectomania

DATE & LOCATION: 1995 June–August, Croydon Museum, London, England

TARGET AUDIENCE: General public

TYPE OF STAND: One-off

SIZE (SQUARE METRES OR FEET): 220m

DESIGNER: Axiom Design Partnership, Surrey, England

STAND MANUFACTURER: Hytex Communication Services Ltd

CLIENT'S BRIEF: To display fifty wildly differing collections from local people – a 'people's show'. The exhibition had to cope with literally thousands of individual items, all of great value to their owners

DESIGN RATIONALE: The design developed from a 'through the keyhole' idea, lead visitors down a

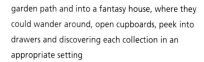

garden path and into a fantasy house, where they could wander around, open cupboards, peek into drawers and discovering each collection in an appropriate setting

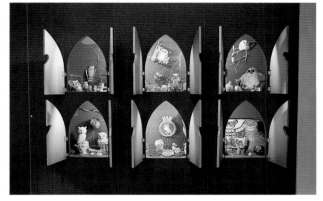

Minnesota Valley National Wildlife Refuge Visitor Center

DATE & LOCATION: 1990, United States Fish and Wildlife Service, Bloomfield, Minnesota, USA

TARGET AUDIENCE: General public

TYPE OF STAND: Permanent

SIZE (SQUARE METRES OR FEET): 10,000ft

DESIGNER: Bruce Burdick, Susan K. Burdick/The Burdick Group, San Francisco, California, USA

CLIENT'S BRIEF: To inform the public about wildlife management issues. To illustrate how visitors can have a positive and negative impact on ecosystem management

DESIGN RATIONALE: Interactive exhibits and computer programmes were used to involve visitors in wildlife management issues, allowing them to participate in a variety of decision making processes. Exhibit areas were devoted to the different ecosystems found in the Minnesota Valley grasslands, wetlands, forests and rivers

PHOTOGRAPHY: George Heinrich, Minneapolis, Minnesota, USA

Ijmuiden
Information Centre

DATE & LOCATION: 1992 Ijmuiden, The Netherlands

TARGET AUDIENCE: General public, tourists

TYPE OF STAND: Permanent

DESIGNER: BRS Premsela Vonk, Amsterdam, The Netherlands

CLIENT'S BRIEF: To construct a visitor centre at one of the world's largest locks. To provide an informative and historical account of the technology used

DESIGN RATIONALE: This was achieved by means of simple display panels and television screens clearly illustrating the workings of old and modern technology

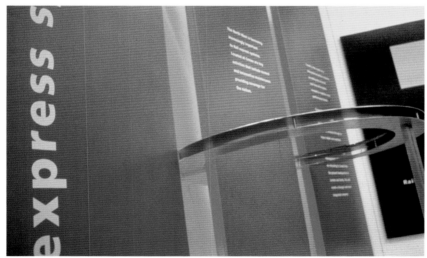

Regional Development Transport and the Environment – Towards the Millennium/Rail Express Systems

DATE & LOCATION: Manchester Airport, England

TARGET AUDIENCE: Corporate

TYPE OF STAND: Modular

SIZE (SQUARE METRES OR FEET): Variable 40-250ft

DESIGNER: Chris Dewar Dixon, Gregor Jackson/Four IV, London, England

STAND MANUFACTURER: Metric 3, England

CLIENT'S BRIEF: To construct a modular and flexible kit, to give a strong confident corporate image however assembled

DESIGN RATIONALE: A multifunctional assembly unit was created, one component could be used as a simple backdrop or every element as a centre piece Arresting text and images were presented on etched acrylic and silk screened panels. Dramatic lighting enhanced an eye-catching powered rail track mounted on a steel ring with moving models of the RES rolling stock

Supermarket of Style

DATE & LOCATION: 1994, The Old Leopolda Railway
Station, Florence, Italy

TARGET AUDIENCE: General public

TYPE OF STAND: One-off

DESIGNER: Italo Lupi/Italo Lupi, Italy in collaboration
with Michele Indovina

CLIENT'S BRIEF: To exhibit international street style
fashions from 1940s to 1990s

DESIGN RATIONALE: Using a station as a display area
meant that the public became part of the
exhibition. A natural thoroughfare, the station,
provided the perfect backdrop to highlight the
movement of youth fashion over 50 years

RESEARCHER: Ted Polhemus

Tradition and New Techniques

DATE & LOCATION: 1992, Paris Industrial Design School, Paris, France

TARGET AUDIENCE: General public

TYPE OF STAND: One-off

SIZE (SQUARE METRES OR FEET): 200m

DESIGNER: Michael Dowd, London, England

STAND MANUFACTURER: Dimensions

CLIENT'S BRIEF: To show the original poster designs of 12 of Japan's leading graphic designers. This was the first exhibition in the glazed courtyard of the new French school of industrial design

DESIGN RATIONALE: The posters were displayed in layers, several posters being visible at the same time. The floor layout was on the pinball principle, floor lights acted as markers sending the visitor through the display. Overhead lighting was employed to avoid shadows on the posters

Live and Let's Spy – Who was the real 'Q'?/English Heritage

DATE & LOCATION: 1993 April, Dover Castle, Kent, England

TARGET AUDIENCE: Children eight years upwards

TYPE OF STAND: Temporary

SIZE (SQUARE METRES OR FEET): 95m

DESIGNER: Furneaux Stewart, London, England

STAND MANUFACTURER: Early Action Group, England

CLIENT'S BRIEF: To reconstruct the exciting environment of World War II espionage in an entertaining way

DESIGN RATIONALE: The exhibition was entered through a gun-barrel, simulating the opening sequence of a James Bond film. Visitors were invited to become agent 0012 and find the real 'Q'. Each area illustrated Charles Fraser-Smith's four principles of espionage. His unique collection of devices were displayed in specially designed back-lit acrylic bubbles on graphic backdrops for close viewing

Power in Partnerships
Exhibition/Food Services of
America

DATE & LOCATION: 1993 March, Scottsdale, Arizona, USA

TARGET AUDIENCE: Food service vendors

TYPE OF STAND: One-off

SIZE (SQUARE METRES OR FEET): Approximately 300ft

DESIGNER: Jack Anderson, David Bates, Cliff Chung, Scott Eggers, Leo Raymundo/Hornall Anderson

Design Works, Seattle, Washington, USA

STAND MANUFACTURER: The Graphics Company, USA

CLIENT'S BRIEF: To focus on a theme symbolising "partnerships". To create a dynamic, exciting and bold display

DESIGN RATIONALE: The star is a reference to the FSA logo and is made up of loose 'energy bursts'. These symbolise the FSA partners. Eight food service technology related icons were created to continue the themes of food service communication and partnership

Boldly into Tomorrow Exhibition/Food Services of America

DATE & LOCATION: 1992 March, Scottsdale, Arizona, USA

TARGET AUDIENCE: Food service vendors

TYPE OF STAND: One-off

SIZE (SQUARE METRES OR FEET): Approximately 5,000ft

DESIGNER: Jack Anderson, Cliff Chung, Jani Drewfs/Hornall Anderson Design Works, Seattle, Washington, USA

CLIENT'S BRIEF: To portray a combined theme of locale and partnership. To provide graphics that would boldly express the idea of unity and team working

DESIGN RATIONALE: An arc, half white, half black, representing the energy transformation of lightning and rain was supported by 'Inca Men' symbolic of the locale. This was set against a backdrop of vibrant colours

ILLUSTRATORS: David Bates, Brian O'Neill/Hornall Anderson, Seattle, Washington

GRAPHICS: HOW-Mac, Seattle, Washington

SIGNAGE: Popich Sign Company, Seattle, Washington

TEXTILES Avita Textiles, Seattle, Washington

Tomorrow's Partnerships Today/Food Services of America

DATE & LOCATION: 1994 March, Scottsdale, Arizona, USA

TARGET AUDIENCE: Food service vendors

TYPE OF STAND: One-off

SIZE (SQUARE METRES OR FEET): 6,400ft

DESIGNER: Jack Anderson, Bruce Branson-Meyer, Cliff Chung, Scott Eggers, Leo Raymundo/Hornall Anderson Design Works, Seatlle, Washington, USA

STAND MANUFACTURER: Dillon Works, USA

CLIENT'S BRIEF: To focus on the locale, making use of the south western colours to symbolise the conference's overall theme

DESIGN RATIONALE: Warm south western colours, an 8ft high cactus and adobe rock wall designs were used to emphasise the locale. The focus was on the use of petroglyph symbols as the conference's logotype and icons

VE Day

DATE & LOCATION: 1995 May, Hyde Park, London,
England

TARGET AUDIENCE: 250,000 members of the general
public

TYPE OF STAND: One-off

SIZE (SQUARE METRES OR FEET): 270m

DESIGNER: Jonathan Park/Fisher Park, London,
England

STAND MANUFACTURER: Unusual Services Ltd, England

CLIENT'S BRIEF: To create a peace feature for the VE
Day commemoration and celebrations in Hyde Park

DESIGN RATIONALE: The peace globe symbolised
worldwide 'Peace, Reconciliation and Hope', with
countries of the world picked out in the fresh
blooms of their national flowers. The public passed
through the rotating globe, viewed a 'Starmap' of a
starry night sky and then signed a commemorative
peace book

ART DIRECTOR Michael Parker

GLOBE SUPPLIER: Impact Structures Ltd

FLOWERS: Barbara Tocher

INTERIOR: Scena Productions

LIGHTING CONTRACTORS Robert Ornbo

STARMAP: Blackout

Divining House

DATE & LOCATION: 1986–1987 Federal Reserve Plaza, Cincinnati, Ohio, USA

TARGET AUDIENCE: General public

TYPE OF STAND: Temporary

SIZE (SQUARE METRES OR FEET): 76m

DESIGNER: Alan Baer, New York, USA

STAND MANUFACTURER: Bill Donnelly and Robert Fry

CLIENT'S BRIEF: To create an exhibition where the roles of the artist and architect are redefined. To make the public aware of untapped sources often scorned by academics and scientists

DESIGN RATIONALE: Divining House is one of three outdoor site installations. Jan Harrison's work is based on the conscious and unconscious parts of the psyche. A paradigm of this juxtaposition is the relationship between humans and animals. The name, Diving House, derives its name from the diving rod thus metaphorically linking previously unresolved elements of being

ARTIST: Jan Harrison

FUNDING: The New York Works Program of the Ohio Arts Council

PHOTOGRAPHER: Ron Forth

VOLUNTEERS: Fifty friends whose assistance and support helped realise this project

CHAPTER FOUR

TRAVELLING

The Age of Optimism

DATE & LOCATION: 1994 February, launched at Millbank
Tower, London, England

TARGET AUDIENCE: General public

TYPE OF STAND: Modular

SIZE (SQUARE METRES OR FEET): 50m

Stand Manufacturer: BBA Graphics

DESIGNER: Furneaux Stewart, London, England

CLIENT'S BRIEF: To celebrate the best English buildings
of the post-war years and explain the need to
conserve and protect them

DESIGN RATIONALE: Varying sizes of folding panels were
used to display explanatory texts and photography.
The stand was designed as a modular system for
easy installation and transport

Amtico/Decorex '93

DATE & LOCATION: 1993 October, Syon Park, London, England

TARGET AUDIENCE: Quality domestic customers and retailers

SIZE (SQUARE METRES OR FEET): 36m

DESIGNER: Adam Rawls/Adam Rawls Associates, London, England

STAND MANUFACTURER: The Amtico Company

CLIENT'S BRIEF: To provide an exceptional design for Decorex '93 allowing Amtico to confirm its position as market leader in luxury vinyl flooring

DESIGN RATIONALE: The stand was presented as a modern art gallery in a low key manner so as to focus visitors' attention on the 'works of art' - the Amtico floors. Using modern art images, the product's creative potential along with the practical and technical precision possibilities were illustrated using CAD/CAM facilities

Look Hear,
Art and Science of the Ear

DATE & LOCATION: 1995 April–September, The Wellcome Centre for Medical Science, London, England

TARGET AUDIENCE: General public

TYPE OF STAND: One-off (but designed to travel)

SIZE (SQUARE METRES OR FEET): 100m

DESIGNER: Charlotte Ross, Andy Thomas, Terry Trickett/Trickett Associates, London, England

CLIENT'S BRIEF: To create an exhibition at the centre's new premises in London devoted to the art and science of the ear. Under the title 'Look Hear', the exhibition follows the path that sound takes through the ear

DESIGN RATIONALE: Through the presentation of light and electron microscopic images, 'Look Hear' enabled visitors to gain an increased understanding of the mechanisms of hearing. The exhibition also provided an opportunity for a group of artists from Bristol to explore the micro-architecture of the ear and present their discoveries to the public

PHOTOGRAPHER: Ian McKinnell

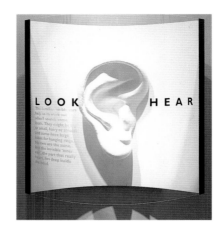
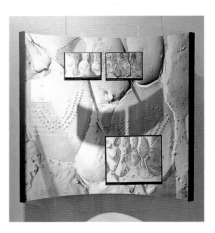

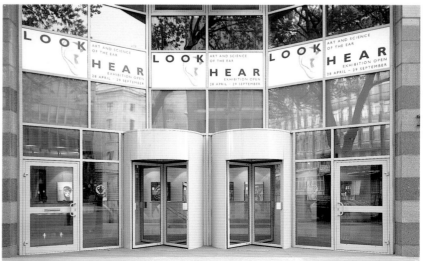

Polyrey

DATE & LOCATION: 1995 May, Koln Messe, Cologne,
Germany

TARGET AUDIENCE: Trade

TYPE OF STAND: Travelling

SIZE (SQUARE METRES OF FEET): 220m

STAND MANUFACTURER: Bartson-Devos, Germany

DESIGNER: Nick Butcher, Stuart Hunter, Kenny
Laurenson/Fitch, London, England

CLIENT'S BRIEF: To create a stand to communicate
Polrey's strength and display new laminate finishes
and collections

DESIGN RATIONALE: The stand reflected the unique
synthesis between emotional needs and technical
solutions by grouping together the new finishes on
a 'new product' wall whilst illustrating the technical
expertise on another

PHOTOGRAPHER: Chris Gascoigne

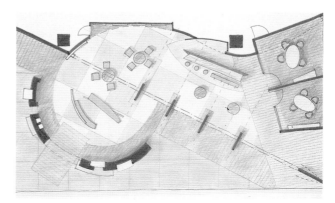

Vidal Sassoon 50th Anniversary Exhibition

DATE & LOCATION: 1992 May, launched in London, England

TARGET AUDIENCE: Trade, media and public relations

TYPE OF STAND: Travelling

SIZE (SQUARE METRES OR FEET): 60m

STAND MANUFACTURER: Central Display, England/Phillips Photographic, England

DESIGNER: 3D Design: Association of Ideas, London, England; Graphic design: The Partners, England

CLIENT'S BRIEF: To create an international exhibition chronicling the 'Life and Work of Vidal Sassoon The

Man'. To support worldwide product launches and develop maximum PR and media coverage

DESIGN RATIONALE: The word 'Sassoon' was writ large and each letter took a particular theme of fashion, people, events relating to Vidal Sassoon and his career. Text panels were interchangeable and in two languages. The number '50' was integrated in the name and finished in gold

COPYWRITER: Beryl McAlhone

PHOTOGRAPHER: Matthew Weinrib

PROJECT MANAGER: Hugh Adlington/P&G

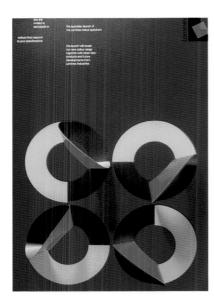

Laminex

DATE & LOCATION: 1990, Australia state capital cities

TARGET AUDIENCE: Interior designers and architects

SIZE (SQUARE METRES OR FEET): 1-3m

STAND MANUFACTURER: Exhibit A, Australia

DESIGNER: Cato Design Inc, Richmond, Victoria, Australia

CLIENT'S BRIEF: To update Laminex's corporate identity. To bring Laminex out of kitchen and alongside the existing DIY and cabinet makers' market. To display the new product and colour range

DESIGN RATIONALE: The exhibition illustrated the diverse range of uses and application of the products. Through the use of twenty three-dimensional sculptures, over sixty finishes were higlighted. The exhibition successfully demonstrated how the base sheet material is transformed into 3-D

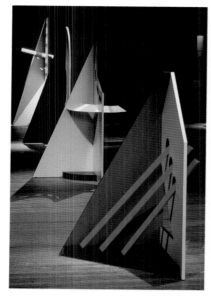

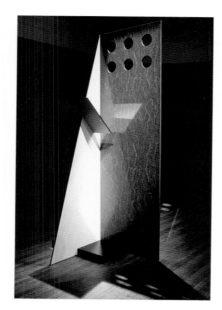

(continued from pp 196–7, Laminex, Australia)

JBL On-Board/Comdex '94

DATE & LOCATION: 1994, Las Vegas, USA

TARGET AUDIENCE: Multimedia market, consumer electronics

TYPE OF STAND: Travelling

SIZE (SQUARE METRES OR FEET): approximately 350m

STAND MANUFACTURER: Farmington Displays Inc, Aperture, USA

DESIGNER: Jane Brady, Mike Mooney, Ben Segal, Christian Uhl/Fitch Inc, Boston, USA

CLIENT'S BRIEF: To create a booth launching JBL onto the multimedia market making use of an existing insulated sound room. To incorporate three existing demonstration areas; an eight-seater cinema, sound demonstration area and an arcade of multimedia podiums

DESIGN RATIONALE: The three areas were linked to present a cohesive identity; the cinema recorded JBL's history, the semi-enclosed, free-standing podiums demonstrated applications such as home multimedia and video games. The graphics conveyed the power and dynamic range of surround sound and provided an appropriate backdrop to the show

Time Out

DATE & LOCATION: 1992 Ministry of Justice, The Hague, The Netherlands

TARGET AUDIENCE: Youth, aged between 16-26 years

SIZE (SQUARE METRES OR FEET): 150m

DESIGNER: René van Raalte

CLIENT'S BRIEF: To convey the concept of the time that is wasted in jail

DESIGN RATIONALE: The inexorability of justice is expressed in a central corridor which consists of a number of door frames. When passing, the electronic 'doors' are 'shut' behind the visitor

ElectroGIG/Siggraph '94

DATE & LOCATION: 1994 July, Orlando, Florida, USA

TARGET AUDIENCE: Electronic imaging companies

SIZE (SQUARE METRES OR FEET): 650m

DESIGNER: Tom van den Haspel/Inizio Group bv, Amsterdam, The Netherlands

CLIENT'S BRIEF: To build a stage suitable for live and computer generated activity and large enough TV for filming. It had to feature ElectroGIG computer programmes, broadcasting and pica equipment separately

DESIGN RATIONALE: Representing a closed box, the stand had three entrances, a ground and first floor. A computer island was installed in three corners of the ground floor and a giant video wall occupied the fourth corner. The centre section was reserved for shows. The stand's high-tech construction was covered by cloth printed with images generated by ElectroGIG equipment and could be dismantled

Makropak Fair '94/ Packaging Unwrapped

DATE & LOCATION: 1994 May, Jaarbeurs, Utrecht, The Netherlands

TARGET AUDIENCE: Packaging industry

SIZE (SQUARE METRES OR FEET): 864m

DESIGNER Tom van den Haspel/Inizio bv, Amsterdam, The Netherlands

CLIENT'S BRIEF: To design a stand incorporating the themes: marketing, the environment, branding, industrial and graphic design

DESIGN RATIONALE: The stand represented an industrial storage system. The bottom section being a general exhibition area, the middle section was reserved for young innovative Dutch art and design students and the upper section contained bulk packaging materials

Por Narices

DATE: 1995

TARGET AUDIENCE: General public

TYPE OF STAND: Travelling

DESIGNER: Vilaseca/Altarriba, Barcelona, Spain

CLIENT'S BRIEF: To create and exhibition to explain the complex workings of the olfactory system

DESIGN RATIONALE: Many hands-on installations allowed the audience to participate. For example: the visitors are invited to smell a tube containing a special essence which does not lose its smell intensity. Other audiovisual and interactive displays with texts panels help explain the exhibits

European Bank for Reconstruction and Development Exhibition Book

DATE & LOCATION: 1993, March, European Bank, London, England

TARGET AUDIENCE: Businessmen, politicians

TYPE OF STAND: Travelling

SIZE (SQUARE METRES OR FEET): 21m

STAND MANUFACTURER: Felix Baumsteiger

DESIGNER: Williams & Phoa, London, England

CLIENT'S BRIEF: To create a display that was flexible enough to be used in both restricted and large spaces. To communicate the basic facts about the bank and its activities

DESIGN RATIONALE: An oversized book presented on a lectern contained all the information of the books displayed, each option on a different spread. Each spread covered a single topic

ADDITIONAL CREDITS: Konu & Morrow

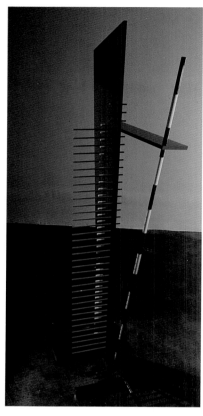

Carmen Furniture Pty Ltd

DATE AND LOCATION: 1992, Designers Saturday,
Melbourne, Victoria, Australia

TARGET AUDIENCE: Architects and interior designers,
specifiers of office furniture systems

STAND MANUFACTURER: Consolidated Graphics,
Australia

DESIGNER: Garry Emery/Emery Vincent Design, South
Melbourne, Australia

CLIENT'S BRIEF: To design directional signs, temporary
furniture and units enhancing the showroom
interior. To display promotional material and have a
food service area

DESIGN RATIONALE: Units were created in a minimalist
style using primary colours to give a thoroughly
modern feel without detracting from the functional
element

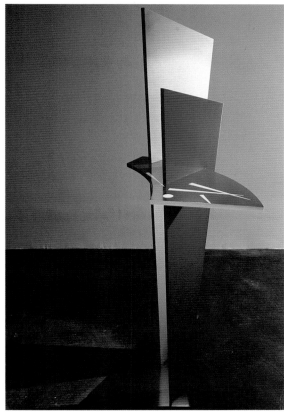

CHAPTER FIVE

MODULAR

Les Grands Projects/Architectures Capitales à Paris

DATE & LOCATION: 1989–1994, launched in New Delhi, Bombay, India

TARGET AUDIENCE: General public

SIZE (SQUARE METRES OR FEET): 1,200m

DESIGNER: Michael Dowd, London, England

STAND MANUFACTURER: Dimensions, England

CLIENT'S BRIEF: To serve as a focus for architectural discussion and debate. To design a practical stand to display models, drawings and photographs whilst meeting safety standards

DESIGN RATIONALE: Individual display units can be stored and transported flat in a stable, vertical position to use as a climbing frame to fix overhead lighting and panel units. The exhibition included audiovisual presentations, a discussion area using classic French café furniture, space-defining screens with panoramic views and an illuminated floor map of Paris

EXHIBITION CURATOR: Groupe 7, France

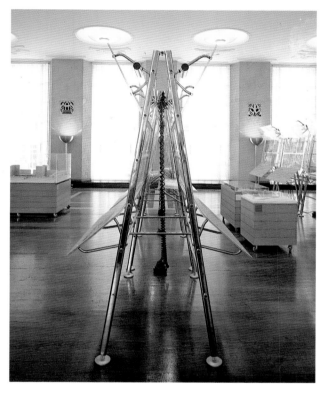

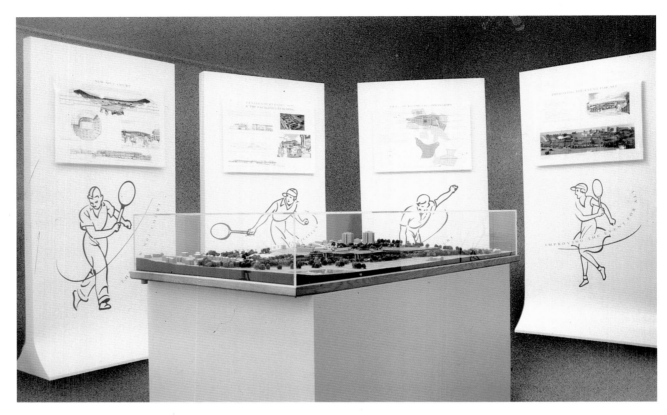

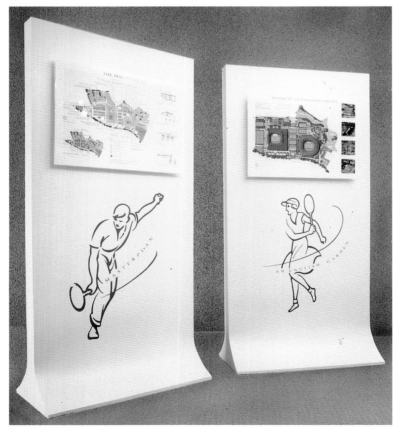

AELTEC Redevelopment/All England Lawn Tennis & Croquet Club

DATE & LOCATION: 1994 June-July, Wimbledon, England

TARGET AUDIENCE: General public

TYPE OF STAND: Travelling

SIZE (SQUARE METRES OR FEET): Variable

DESIGNER: Richard Dragun, Jo Walsh/BDP Design, London, England

STAND MANUFACTURER: Autograph Exhibitions, England

CLIENT'S BRIEF: To describe the proposed redevelopment of Number One Court and associated facilities

DESIGN RATIONALE: Self-supporting panels were designed. The splayed base provided a solid foot that echoed the sweeping movements of the 'tennis players' employed to illustrate the title of each section

PHOTOGRAPHER: David Barbour

FSS, Sistema de Señalización Móvil

DATE & LOCATION: Spain

TARGET AUDIENCE: Designers, architects, museums, facility managers

TYPE OF STAND: Kit form

SIZE (SQUARE METRES OR FEET): 0.33-2m

DESIGNER: HB Sign Company, London, England

CLIENT'S BRIEF: To provide a free standing sign system on which information can be easily displayed

DESIGN RATIONALE: An interchangeable set of boards with aluminium aerofoil stands were designed. Information can be displayed between two sheets of glass or on base of vinyl plastic board to be used as special pin or magnet board

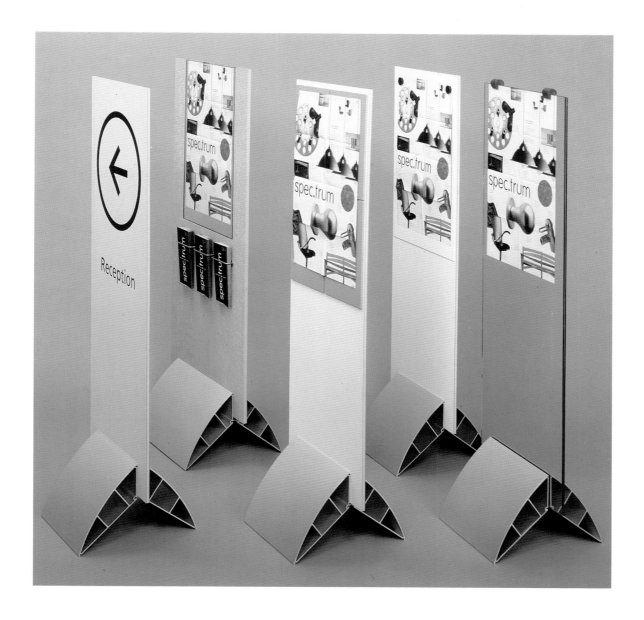

The New Designers' Exhibition

DATE & LOCATION: 1995 July, Business Design Centre, London, England

TARGET AUDIENCE: Low turnover business and companies

SIZE (SQUARE METRES OR FEET): 24m

DESIGNER: Jamie Douglas/De Montfort University, Leicester, England

STAND MANUFACTURER: Rexham, Leicester, England

CLIENT'S BRIEF: To design an exhibition stand specific for the new designers show, to allow as many students to exhibit as possible, to stay within a low budget yet still remain professional

DESIGN RATIONALE: The cardboard structure was chosen for its cost effectiveness. It is easily transported, light weight and simple to erect, a relatively inexpensive option for corporate display

Wellcome

DATE & LOCATION: 1994 December, The Wellcome Centre for Medical Science, London, England

TARGET AUDIENCE: Visitors and in-house staff

TYPE OF STAND: Modular

SIZE (SQUARE METRES OR FEET): 12m

DESIGNER: Andrew Thomas, Terry Trickett/Trickett Associates, London, England

STAND MANUFACTURER: Exhibition Image, Scott Howard, England

CLIENT'S BRIEF: To provide displays on three office floors, information on aspects of the Centre's current work whilst including references to the past and provide insights into the future

DESIGN RATIONALE: Displays were located within the lift lobbies and contained specific images which reflected the work of the departments located on each floor. The chrome steel framework of the displays enabled selected 'key' images to be illuminated

PHOTOGRAPHER: Richard Bryant/Arcaid, England

National Power
Electrotech Stand

DATE & LOCATION: 1994 June, Electrotech '94, National
Exhibition Centre, Birmingham, England

TARGET AUDIENCE: Specialist trade, international power
authorities:

TYPE OF STAND: Modular

SIZE (SQUARE METRES OR FEET): 100m

DESIGNER: Furneaux Stewart, London, England

CLIENT'S BRIEF: To use a system that incorporated the
latest lighting, graphic and construction technology

DESIGN RATIONALE: The system combined
choreographed and integrated cross fades, and
pulsing light-emitting diodes to convey messages in
a format that is literally energised by the flow of
electricity. The result is a highly adaptable
construction allowing great flexibility to be used at
any event

GRAPHICS: BBA Graphics, England

Newbridge Networks Ltd/Networld Interop

DATE & LOCATION: 1994 June, Berlin, Germany

TARGET AUDIENCE: Networking managers

TYPE OF STAND: Modular

SIZE (SQUARE METRES OR FEET): 120m

DESIGNER: Innervisions Interiors & Exhibitions Ltd, London, England

CLIENT'S BRIEF: To design a flexible, modular exhibit which reflected the new brand

DESIGN RATIONALE: Elements of the new branding were incorporated in a three-dimensional way into the architecture of the stand design. The key feature was an inverted cone and fan-shaped ceiling

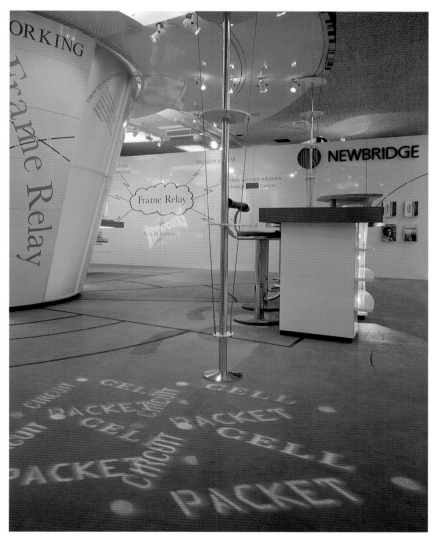

Index of Projects

Directory of Practising Designers

2LK Design
2 St. George's Yard, Castle Street,
Farnham, Surrey GU9 7LW, UK
PROJECT: Sony Broadcast &
Professionals Europe/
International Broadcasting
Convention 82–3

Association of Ideas
15 The Coda Centre, 189 Munster
Road, London SW6 6AW, UK
PROJECT: Vidal Sassoon 50th
Anniversary Exhibition 194–5

Adams Rawls Associates
7 Tideway Yard, 125 Mortlake High
Street, London SW14 8SN, UK
PROJECT: Amtico/Decorex '93 189

Alan Baer
34 Hunter Street, Kingston,
NY 12401, USA
PROJECTS: Vital Gesture: Franz Kline in
Retrospect (The) 70; Galleries Devoted
to the Arts of Africa and the Americas
71; Divining House 185

Alan Irvine Architects
1 Aubrey Place, London NW6 9BH, UK
PROJECT: Science in the Eighteenth
Century 54–5

Axiom Design Partnership
6 Raleigh Drive, Claygate,
Surrey KT10 9DE, UK
PROJECT: Collectomania 170–1

BDP Design
P.O. Box 4WD, 19 Gresse Street,
London W1A 4WD, UK
PROJECT: AELTEC Redevelopment/All
England Lawn Tennis and Croquet
Club 214

BRS Premsela Vonk
Nieuwe, Prinsengracht 89, 1018 VR,
Amsterdam, The Netherlands
PROJECT: Time Out 202; Treasure
Chamber 42; North Sea Exhibition 46–7;
Herman Miller/Orgatec '94 92–3;
Enkhuizen Historical Museum 166–7;
Ijmuiden Information Centre 174

Burdick Group (The)
35 South Park, San Francisco, CA
94107, USA
PROJECTS: Philips Competence Centre
154–7; Information Superhighway
Exhibit/Oracle Corporation 158–9;
Minnesota Valley National Wildlife
Refuge Visitor Center 172–3

Carter Wong & Partners
29 Brook Mews North, London W2 3BW
PROJECT: All Change, Russian Avant-
garde Books 1912–1934 50–1

Cartlidge Levene
Level Three, 101 Goswell Road,
London EC1V 7ER, UK
PROJECTS: Jacobsen Retrospective
Design Museum 43; Review Gallery
Design Museum 44–5; thinkteck/TDN
(Tokyo Design Network) 64–5

Cato Design Inc.
254 Swan Street, Richmond,
Victoria 3121, Australia
PROJECT: Laminex 196–9

Checkland Kindleysides
Fowke Street, Rothley, Leicester,
Leicestershire LE7 7PJ, UK
PROJECT: Astra/Cable and Satellite '95
86–7

Conceptor International
Tooley Street, London SE1 2TU, UK
PROJECTS: Dockyard Apprentice (The)
168–9; Tower Bridge 'The Celebration
Story'/World Travel Market 115

Drenttel Doyle Partners
1123 Broadway, 25th Street, New
York, NY 10010, USA
PROJECT: Architecture of New Prague
(The) 48–9

Emery Vincent Design
80 Market Street, South Melbourne,
Victoria 3205, Australia
PROJECTS: Powerhouse Museum 29;
Amcor Ltd 144–7; Carmen Furniture
Pty Ltd 208–9; Governor Phillip Tower
148–9

Fisher Park
12 Whidborne Street,
London WC1H 8EU, UK
PROJECT: VE Day 184

Fitch
Commonwealth House,
Number One, New Oxford Street,
London WC1E 1WW, UK
PROJECTS: Seapower in the Twentieth
Century 38–9; Health Matters 36–7;
Polyrey 192–3; Iomega Booth/
Comdex '94 88–9; JBL/Live '94 110–1;
JBL On-Board/
Comdex '94 200–1; Svoboda/Orgatex
'94 100–1

Formpur
Industriestrasse 15, D-72585 Riederich,
Germany
PROJECT: Firma Nemetschek/CEBIT '95
84–5

Four IV
1 St. Peter's Street, London N1 8JD, UK
PROJECT: Regional Development
Transport and the Environment –
Towards the Millennium/Rail Express
Systems 175

Frankfurt Balkind Partners
244 East 58th Street, New York, NY
10022, USA
PROJECT: HBJ Treasury of Literature
Exhibit 126–7

Furneaux Stewart
16E Portland Road, Holland Park,
London W11 4LA, UK
PROJECTS: Storage Works/CEBIT '94
112–3; Citroën Ulster Show Stand
134–5; National Power Electrotech
Stand 216–9; Age of Optimism (The)
188; Live and Let's Spy – Who Was the
Real 'Q'?/
English Heritage 180; BT Goonhilly
Visitor Centre 163; Porsche
Motorshow Stand 140–1

Giant
A1 Riverside, Metropolitan Wharf,
Wapping Wall, London E1 9SS, UK
PROJECT: Kuwait Petroleum
Lubricants/March '92 107

Harper Mackay Ltd
33–37 Charterhouse Square,
London EC1M 6EA, UK
PROJECT: Mazda Stand 138–9

HB Sign Company (The)
120 Kings Road, Chelsea,
London SW3 4TR, UK
PROJECT: FSS, Sistema de Señalización
Móvil 215

HG Créations
11 rue Heinrich, 92100 Boulogne,
France
PROJECT: Citroën/Salon International
de l'Automobile 132–3

Hornall Anderson Design Works
1008 Western Avenue, Suite 600,
Seattle, Washington 98104, USA
PROJECTS: AGI Exhibition/AGI 94;
Tomorrow's Partnerships Today/Food
Services of America 183; Boldly into
Tomorrow Exhibition/Food Services of
America 182; Power in Partnerships

Exhibition/Food Services of America
181; Intermation/Corporation
Intermation Exhibition 106

Imagination
25 Store Street, South Crescent,
London WC1E 7BL, UK
PROJECTS: BT/Innovation '94 120–1;
Fantasy Factory/
Cadbury Ltd 96–7

Ingo Maurer GmbH
Kaiserstrasse 47, 80801 Munich,
Germany
PROJECT: Porca Miseria!–Light in the
Tunnel 78–9

Inizio Group bv
Ditlaar 1, 1066 EE, Amsterdam,
The Netherlands
PROJECTS: Packaging
Unwrapped/Makropak Fair '94 204–5;
ElectroGIG/Siggraph '94 203

**Innervisions Interiors &
Exhibitions Ltd**
No. 1 Primrose Mews, 1A Sharpleshall
Street, London NW1 8YW, UK
PROJECTS: Newbridge Networks
Ltd/Networld Interop '94 220–1; IBM
90; Philips Electronics/Live '94 98–9;
Intel Beacon '95 102–3; Compaq
Computer Network '94 124–5;
Acclaim Entertainment Ltd/Future
Entertainment 122–3; Reuters/Forex
'94 118–9; Monotype Systems Ltd 91;
Peugeot Talbot Motor
Company/International Motorshow
'94 136–7; Intel (Europe) GmbH/CeBit
'93 104–5; Apple Computer/
Apple Expo '94 108–9

Italo Lupi
39 Via Vigevamo, 20144 Milan, Italy
PROJECTS: Renaissance, the
Performance of Architecture 52–3;
Supermarket of Style 176–7;
BTicino 128–9

James Gardner: 3D Concepts Ltd
Studio, Haverstock Hill,
London NW3 2AY, UK
PROJECT: Human Intolerance and its
Consequence 20–1

**Jamie Douglas, De Montfort
University, Leicester, England**
61 Beaconsfield Road, Leicester,
Leicestershire LE3 0FG, UK
PROJECT: New Designers' Exhibition
(The) 216

Jasper Jacobs Associates
33 Rathbone Place,
London W1P 1AD, UK
PROJECT: Health Matters 36–7

Land Design Studio Ltd
14 Barley Mow Passage, Chiswick,
London W4 4PH
PROJECT: Secret War 72–3

MET Studio Ltd
6–8 Standard Place, Rivington Street,
London EC2A 3BE, UK
PROJECTS: Evolution House 28; MET
Studio/Cruise and Ferry '95 114;
Environment Theatre (The) 26–7;
Science for Life 32–5; Life Sciences
Gallery 30–1

MICE Group plc
11 Calico Row, Plantation Wharf,
York Road, Wandsworth,
London SW11 3TW, UK
PROJECT: Sony/Live '94 116–7

Michael Dowd
14 Stevenson Way, London NW1, UK
PROJECTS: Tradition and New
Techniques 178–9; Les Grands
Projets/Architectures Capitales à Paris
212–3

**Muséographica Mexico and
Créations publicitaires Moser SA**
c/o Olympic Museum, Quay d'Ouchy 1,
P.O. Box 1001, Lausanne, Switzerland
PROJECT: Cycloramas: Summer Olympic
Games & Winter Olympic Games 24–5

Nigel Simpkins Design
70 Tib Street, Manchester M4 1LG, UK
PROJECT: Pumphouse: People's History
Museum 60–1

Northcross
Waterside House, 46 The Shore, Leith,
Edinburgh EH6 6QU, UK
PROJECT: Phonehouse/Direct Line
Insurance plc 95

Opera Ruimtelijk Ontwerpers
Sarphatistraat 29, 1018 EV
Amsterdam, The Netherlands
PROJECTS: 'Broken Lines' 22–3; 'Keep
out of the Cold . . . Clothing for Arctic
Dwellers' 40–1

Pippo Lionni & Associates
14 rue Kléber, 93100 Montreuil, Paris,
France
PROJECT: Fragile: Espace jeunes
créateurs/Design miroir du siècle/IKEA
76–7

Roger Pfund
c/o International Red Cross and Red
Crescent Museum, 17 avenue de la
Paix, CH 1202, Geneva, Switzerland
PROJECT: Pictures for Fighting Aids 56

Ronayne Design
17 Manor Avenue, London SE4 1PE, UK
PROJECT: Rochester Guild Hall
Museum/Rochester-upon-Medway City
Council 150–1

Sawaya & Moroni Spa
Sede Legale, Piazza Missori 2, 20122,
Milano, Italy
PROJECT: Argento è Luce 150–1

Stanton Williams
10 Huguenot Place, Heneage Street,
London E1 5LJ, UK
PROJECTS: Birmingham Gas Hall (The)
62–3; Art of Ancient Mexico (The)
66–9

Total Design
P.O. Box 19420, 1000 GK Amsterdam,
The Netherlands
PROJECT: Ahrend Group/Orgatec '94
130–1

Trickett & Webb
84 Marchmont Street,
London WC1N 1AG, UK
PROJECTS: Computer Cab/Taxi Driver of
the Year 80–1; Channel Islands (The):
Occupation and Liberation, 1940–1945
160–1; Wellcome 217; Look Hear, Art
and Science of the Ear 190–1

Vilaseca/Altarriba Associates
Aribau, 230–240, 50 M, 08006,
Barcelona, Spain
PROJECTS: Por Norices 206; People's
City (The) 152–3

**Watano Matsuzaki
Communications bv**
Entropotdok 58A, 1018 AD,
Amsterdam, The Netherlands
PROJECT: Sons of the Sun and
Daughters of the Moon 57

Williams & Phoa
2a Pear Tree Court, London EC1R 0DS, UK
PROJECT: European Bank for
Reconstruction and Development
Exhibition Book 207

Woodworth Associates
151 Newbury Street, Portland,
Maine 04101, USA
PROJECT: Museum at Portland Head
(The) 162